PRAISE FOR
CATHERINE YAEL SEROTA SHEALY

"I could hear the chuckles grow behind me as people realized what was going to happen. Little Bobby would be proud, and so was I."

—Gwenda Ledbetter, WLOS Story Lady

"I could not stop reading these stories and when I had finished, I wanted more. This is a thoroughly moving and satisfying book. I'm hoping there will be a sequel."

—Geraldine Buckley Elrod, Chaplain, Storyteller, Speaker, Educator

"I'll go anywhere to hear Catherine tell! She paints such vivid pictures. I can see them in my mind."

—Joy Bolt, Jonesborough Storytellers Guild

"Many artists endeavor to capture scenes of Appalachia on canvas, but Catherine paints landscapes with descriptive prose."

—Tim Lowry, Professional Storyteller

AN APPALACHIAN LIFE

A STORYTELLER'S PERSPECTIVE

CATHERINE YAEL SEROTA SHEALY

ISBN: 979-8999569806

Illustrations by Emilie Maino
Produced by Publish Pros | publishpros.com

To My Husband,
Wallace,
who introduced me to storytelling as an art,
is my IT expert
and
My One and Only

My sincerest appreciation to:
Tim Lowry
Wayne Edwards
Gwenda Ledbetter
Kiesa Kay
Debbie Nance
Trish Taylor
Cornelia Roach Serota
Wallace Shealy
John Albert Serota
Walter Frances Burns III
Dr. Greg Perry
Marcy Trott Hawley

CONTENTS

Foreword. vii
Thoughts On Being A Storyteller xi

BEGINNINGS 1

    The Early Years. 3
    Rabbit 15
    Project Management 21
    The Awfulest Christmas Tree 33
    Adventures in Flora and Fauna. 41
    Biscuits 45
    Duck 49
    Life At Mill Pond Farm 55
    Deviant Behaviors 63
    Beyond DC 67

THE LITTLE BOBBY CHRONICLES 77

    Little Bobby and Grandaddy. 79
    Little Bobby and the School Bus. 85
    Little Bobby and the Girl in the Attic Window . 91
    Little Bobby's Summer Vacation Buster 105

A Diversion 113

    We Are So Much Like Them 115

Heritage 121

    The Sin Eater 123
    Madison County, 1969 127
    The Pancake Princess 135
    Wampus Cat 143
    Reuben May 147
    The Packhorse Library Initiative 155
    Cloudland 159
    The Vegetable Mistress 165
    Mr. Burns 171
    Endnote 191
    The Wreath in the Graveyard 193

Jack Tale 199

    Jack out Awhile in the World 201

References 209
About the Author 211

FOREWORD

The title of the last story in this book, "Jack out Awhile in the World," serves as a metaphor for this entire collection and its author. Growing up in the Appalachian Mountains, Catherine Yael Serota Shealy carefully studied the high, craggy peaks, the massive chestnut trees, the diminutive trillium, and the lumbering black bears, not just as objects of curiosity, but more like books in a well-stocked library. She also listened intently to the voices of her family and neighbors, taking in their songs and sayings. She and Jack share the family traits of "big eyes and big ears." And like the folk hero, with an intuition inherited from her ancestors, Catherine knew these treasures should be stored up in the heart until the time when she would go "out awhile in the world."

Some folks would say Jack was "lazy" or "simple," but that could never be said of Catherine. She has always possessed inner drive (read "Project Management"), deep curiosity (read "Adventures in Flora and Fauna"), and plenty of determination (read "Biscuits" and "Duck"). These qualities came naturally and were sharpened by parental guidance and education into effective tools for a very successful professional life and a resume that includes Christmas-tree grower, nurserywoman, mental health therapist, grant writer, Tennessee homesteader, world traveler, and philanthropist. With such an impressive list of accomplishments, some of the home folk might accuse Catherine of "having got above her raising," but I assure you, Appalachia has always been at the very soul of every entrepreneurial undertaking, career move, or charitable project.

Many artists endeavor to capture scenes of Appalachia on canvas, but Catherine paints landscapes with descriptive prose. Her intimate knowledge of farm life and her love of nature is evident in the stories of her own garden at Mill Pond Farm. She so beautifully describes her heirloom long greasy beans that you can almost forgive the thieves who helped themselves to three bushels of her prized crop. The bucolic Schellenberg Farm from the "The Little Bobby Chronicles" with its house and Dutch barn standing at the edge of fields full of silage, sweet corn, alfalfa, and red clover is a pastoral scene that reminds me of a phrase from the poet James Whitcomb Riley. It is "a pictur' that no painter has the colorin' to mock."

Not only does Catherine love the mountain farms, she also equally values the people who work the land. Too many writers, even native Appalachians, create cartoonish hillbilly characters reminiscent of Mammy and Pappy Yokem. Catherine loves her people too much to be guilty of such silliness. She often expresses her affection for hill folk by using colloquial words and phrases that are authentic, but never poke fun or rob people of their dignity. Old-fashioned terms like "folding money" for paper currency and "buster" for a momentous occasion are spot on. I also appreciate Catherine's genuine Appalachian way of describing certain situations. For instance, she does not write "Bobby quietly stepped toward the edge of a group of children," but instead uses the more culturally correct "He fetched up to a knot of boys and girls." These words and phrases help to preserve a regional speech that is nearly gone.

It must be admitted that there are plenty of other writers who can paint word pictures and use mountain dialect to great effect. What makes this book unique is that these stories consistently show how the traditions of love for the land and love for each other serve Appalachians even up to the present day. In a manner of speaking, every one of these stories could be called "Jack out Awhile in the World" because Appalachian natives can take what they know and love and apply it to things that are unfamiliar or even frightening. Consequently, a six-year-old ain't afraid of the big, noisy school bus because he already knows how to handle a rattlesnake. A lady homesteader alone on her mountain farm will figure out how to get through Covid because she learned the stories of ancestors who struggled against tuberculosis. And the local "pancake princess" will one day become a proper opera star because she learned a thing or two about grit and determination growing up in the backwoods of Rocky Pine Valley.

These stories share the secrets of resilience. And for that reason, they should be valued by people everywhere, because just like the folk hero Jack, just like Catherine Shealy, just like everybody else in Appalachia (or any other region for that matter), sooner or later you must go out into the world, and it's best to have stories to sustain you for the journey, for the adventure, for life.

Tim Lowry
Professional Storyteller
Author of *Haunted by Dickens* and *Southern Fried Circus*

THOUGHTS ON BEING A STORYTELLER

1. A storyteller grows with the help of her friends. Friends give you information for stories, sometimes by intention, sometimes by a glancing word or phrase. A request, or one of their memories. A sleeping shirt I have states on the front, "If you have a life, you have a story." I think writing a book later in life gives you a sense of longevity, of having accumulated a little wisdom from interacting with all the beauty and pitfalls of the world.

2. My mentor early on, Gwenda Ledbetter, told me repeatedly: "Pay attention." I learned to use my five senses, becoming attuned to my surroundings. As my sensitivity grew, it went deeper, almost in an emotive, spiritual sense, to feelings and unspoken messages from the past and the universe. I call this process developmental internalization and feedback. It's how I work and create.

3. A timeline of life has space for tucking in stories and fleeting remembrances. For example, passing through Texas last fall, I saw the signs to Denton. The intensity of my first eleven-year-old crush on a second cousin I met during a

family trip there in 1959 rushed back in memory. We exchanged a few letters, then nothing. I wondered what happened to him.

One early spring day years ago, I drove through a wooded area in Boone, North Carolina, and saw a vast carpet of spring beauties and many-colored crocuses spreading down the slope. A very old lady was sitting on a faded garden bench at the bottom. I wondered if she was the person who had started this carpet of beauty at the top of the slope decades before, just so she could sit and remember the passing years as the flowers crept downhill. Moments like these enrich life, and storytellers record and preserve them.

4. Then there is the historical narrative. Taking a snippet of history or the life of a real person and building a plot, characters, and action around it preserves history and makes it so interesting people remember it and learn life lessons.

BEGINNINGS

I was born in Asheville, North Carolina, in 1949, a time when the country had recovered from the Second World War and begun to surge into the most prosperous economy the world has ever known. Simultaneously, the old ways of the people native to the Appalachians were hanging on by a thread. Looking back, I see many folkways, much history, and observations that are valuable and have accompanied me through life. I was a Western North Carolinian for sixty-eight years, becoming an East Tennessean in 2018, but remaining in the mountains. To have been born and grown up in this time, in this place, with these people, I am immensely grateful.

THE EARLY YEARS

Mother and Daddy and I lived in a log house named "Hideaway" on the corner of Old Haw Creek Road and Trinity Chapel Road in the country of eastern Buncombe County. When my mother purchased the property in 1947, it was already eighty years old. The master bedroom, bath, and dining room had been added on twenty years earlier. The kitchen, living room, and my bedroom were original to the structure. At night, small brown bats would swoop down the chimney and over our heads. I think they slept there during the day but were soon evicted when my father installed a mesh screen. I loved our yard, full of mature, ninety-foot-tall white pine, hickory, and oak that produced an abundance of seeds and nuts and fed many small animals. Large rhododendron and azaleas were foundation plantings around the house and bloomed profusely in the spring. The house was well set back from Trinity Chapel, behind the large trees and smaller hemlocks and accessed by a long white gravel drive. A margin of wood bounded the north side to Old Haw Creek Road. A secondary growth forest backed up to the east and south ends of the property. I sat in the warm grass outside the kitchen door with one of Mother's old pots and a big serving spoon and excavated for worms, roly-polys, and beetles. I usually tasted and sometimes ate them, so Mother periodically wormed me. She would catch little ring-neck and garter snakes that lived in the low stone wall encircling the garden, and we would play with them. Inside, I entertained myself by re-potting her houseplants into the upholstered furniture.

There were many delights at Hideaway, but the real excitement lived next door.

Across the tall boxwood hedge and through the woods lived Jack and Vasey Jones, sweet and kind. They had no children and wanted them desperately. After I was born, and my mother returned to teaching at Asheville Biltmore College, they offered childcare. Thus began four wonderful years.

Jack was a timber cruiser and farmer, and Vasey kept house. They lived in a large, beautiful Arts and Crafts home built by Jack's father in the 1910s. The front parlor was decorated in the Victorian style and boasted a massive carved mahogany sofa upholstered in dark garnet velvet and stuffed with horsehair. One's bottom made no dent in those cushions, or in the four, heavy damask-covered club chairs that seemed to encourage upright posture. These pieces were adorned with pure white crocheted antimacassars. I held them up to my face and peeped through the lace. I also liked to drape them over my head. Patient Vasey repeatedly retrieved and returned them to the living room until she crocheted a designated one for me. I wore it when I played dress-up princess in front of the massive hall tree, pirouetting before the eight-foot-tall, beveled mirror. To a two-year-old child, the furniture pieces belonged to a race of giants.

The finest features in the parlor reposed on either side of the fireplace. The twin round, glass-fronted, golden oak curio cabinets caught my eye, for they were filled with dozens and dozens of sparkling treasures— crystal snowflakes, brightly painted little animals, diminutive cups and saucers, commemorative sterling silver spoons, delicate Capodimonte flowers, and even a tiny fox made of real fur! It was impossible for a little girl to resist. First I was warned, then admonished in increasingly stern statements, and finally punished for getting into the cabinets and playing. "Playing" in my lexicon meant taking out and inadvertently breaking the little objects. Several were from Europe, and many of them were irreplaceable. Curiosity got the best of me and I couldn't leave them alone.

Living with Jack and Vasey were Vasey's maiden sisters, Effie and Neely, who shared a bedroom. Her elder sister, Delsey, had married Mr. Head and moved around the corner and three houses up on Old Haw

Creek Road. Neely was secretary to the rector of First Presbyterian, and Effie was head Bookkeeper at Ivey's Department Store in downtown Asheville. The two of them met the bus every morning and had left for town by the time Mother brought me over. Ivey's had a fine gifts department and Mother became a major investor as she paid Effie weekly to purchase items to restock the curio cabinets. Finally, she had enough. A memorable spanking with Mother's pancake turner ended my desire to explore, and thus thwarted, I turned my attention to the outside.

Out behind the house was a large enclosure housing a rooster, several laying hens, and a couple of pink pigs. I chased the hens, who kicked up a cloud of dust and droppings as I pursued them around and around their yard. Vasey told me I would have no cake for dessert if I kept on scaring them too badly to lay eggs. The Jersey milk cow lived in the barn and yearly produced a calf. Mother would pick me up in the late afternoon, and when I returned the next morning, the cow had magically made a little calf! I asked questions. Jack explained the cow had found the baby wandering in the woods and brought it home to raise. That made sense as Mother pointed out raccoon, squirrel, possum, and fox families on our walks in the woods. I knew the woods contained plenty of mysteries that my endless questions had not resolved and lots of magical occurrences. I was just happy the little calf had a mother.

I didn't care for the pigs. They were pushy, smelly, muddy and made nasty snorting sounds. They tried to shove their dirty quivering snouts into my hands and nipped at my fingers with their hard gums. Jack cautioned I should leave them alone as they had been known to trample and eat little children who aggravated them. That surely made an impression, and I backed out of the pig sty. I silently watched Jack eat ham and pork chops. I knew they came from the nasty pigs. My mind ruminated on what he had told me, and I wondered if he was what the National Geographic Magazine called a "candleball." I really didn't think kind Vasey would let the pigs eat children and then Jack would eat the pig meat. I wanted Jack to get a big mean dog to keep those pigs in line. Instead, he brought home a yappy little fox terrier that chased me around the yard, hemmed me up against the house, and peed on my leg.

I loved the dining room with the huge, carved, dark walnut table and its eight ornate high-backed chairs. The other two furniture pieces were the massive eight-foot-tall china cabinet locked against my nosiness and a long carved sideboard where Vasey kept her African violets. Ever-blooming in white, pink, and purple, their lush velvet leaves just begged to be stroked, although I wasn't allowed. The best thing about the sideboard was the footed stands with their tall glass domes. Vasey was a very skilled cook. One stand displayed cakes—spice, six-layered coconut, black walnut, German chocolate, black forest, or a rich, heavy pound cake redolent of butter and vanilla. The other stand proudly held a pie—lattice-topped apple, blueberry, coconut, chocolate, or lemon with high-lofting meringue in toasty deliciousness.

Vasey lovingly served Jack and me. We sat at the table while Vasey stood behind his left shoulder ready to respond to his needs. I never saw her sit down and eat with Jack. Her meals were all served family-style—meats carved decorously on platters and vegetables steaming in deep bowls—and made with ingredients from the garden, smokehouse, freezer, and basement can room. Sometimes my chicken friends met Vasey's chopping block. Coffee perked gently in the kitchen, and sweet milk, lemonade, and buttermilk were at hand.

Jack would rise from the table after dessert, nod to Vasey, and say, "Thank you, ma'am, for that fine meal." He would kiss her cheek and leave the house on his farming duties.

Vasey cleared the table and washed up the dishes. I stood on a stool and "helped." Then she and I would lay across the bed for a story and nap for two hours. Before Mama came for me, I would get a bath and change into the nice clothing I had arrived in that morning. Vasey kept an old set of what she called "play clothes" that I wore during the day, a playsuit brought by Neely from Ivey's.

Mother was bemused by the fact that I was always tidy and clean when she arrived. One day she asked Vasey, "Doesn't Anne Catherine go out and play? I would like her to be outside. She's always so clean!"

Vasey confessed that little Cathy got almost pig-nasty during the day but was cleaned up before Mother got there. She produced the filthy, stiff playsuit that was washed every weekend. I thought Mother would be appalled, but she laughed and told Vasey it was all right to send me home dirty from the day—she would bathe me before supper. Still, Vasey never sent me home dirty; it was a matter of honor and providing good care to let me tear around all day then get cleaned up for Mother.

The garden was a wonderland of an acre proportion. Tall corn, supporting both pole beans and morning glories seemed to scrape the sky. Bush-bean greenery plumped in straight rows next to verdant Kennebeck potato plants. Tops of tomatoes waved over their poles and commingled with the peppers. Vines bearing sweet potatoes, cantaloupes, pumpkins, gourds, and watermelons ran hither and yon under old-fashioned varieties of apple, cherry, and peach trees. The top to a large cold frame made from an old window sash was propped open above lettuce and spinach. Spiky okra shared quarters with squashes, eggplant, turnips, and onions.

A broad flower border ran around the entire garden. It sported tall and dwarf hollyhocks, snapdragons, zinnias, asters, delphinium, and marigolds, yielding vases of cut flowers placed throughout the house. The roadside portion of the garden border displayed Vasey's prize-winning sunflowers and dahlia collection to the world. She showed her dahlias and canned goods at the Buncombe County Fair and sold gourds and pumpkins at the Lexington Avenue Farmers' Market in the fall. She and Jack both cared for and harvested the garden. She called her sales "my butter and egg money." I didn't see how gourds and pumpkins had anything to do with the chickens.

The garden was full of singing birds, butterflies, and hummers flitting like big jewels amongst the blossoms. I chased the butterflies and the rabbits that came to graze in the grassy rows. It was my favorite place for fantasy play, imaging the scarecrow on his stick was my friend. I picked and ate the tender small cucumbers and tomatoes, which were so good! Vasey dried apple and peach rings on a clean window screen outside the kitchen porch and covered them with a soft piece of muslin to discourage hungry birds. Canning and freezing vegetables began in August. In my small way, I attempted to help by stringing and breaking beans as Vasey and I sat on the back porch. In the fall,

I helped harvest seeds, knotting them into cambric cloth squares and tying a paper label to them with a tiny wire.

Before Mother arrived in the afternoon, I reluctantly came inside to be tidied up. There was a little stool in the bathroom made and painted with flowers and butterflies by Jack. I stood on it by the tall pedestal sink or sat in the bathtub as the day's dirt was sponged off. Then I was re-dressed in the spotless outfit I had arrived in hours earlier.

Flour, salt, and baking powder waited in the heavy pink-and-blue-striped bowl under the sifter on the countertop of the white-enameled cupboard. A lump of lard was worked into the dry ingredients with Vasey's hands. A splash of buttermilk, and those hands mixed and kneaded the dough. It was then turned out onto the floured tabletop and folded and patted several times before being cut and placed snugly side by side into the pan. When the biscuits were done, pats of butter from the daisy-imprinted press Jack had hand-carved were lavished onto the halves and eaten with her preserves or syrup or homemade molasses.

A tall, wooden churn with a long-handled dasher sat on the enclosed back porch next to the twenty-pound bucket of Armour's Best Lard. Vasey still made her own butter, skimming the glass jars of Jersey milk of their cream, setting some aside to clabber for bread-making, and pouring the rest into the churn. She sat out on the porch, slapping the dasher up and down and up and down in the churn between her knees while singing hymns or rhythmically reciting from the Psalms. She taught me the Scriptures that way. When the butter was set, we took the dasher into the kitchen to the white enameled sink and scraped the butter into a large aluminum dishpan where it was washed and drained. Then it was pushed and patted to remove all the water and finally packed into the butter press. Sometimes the butter was salted and sometimes left "sweet" for baking. I remember that butter as the best I ever tasted. It came to the dinner table melting in sweet riverlets over lima beans, stewed potatoes, and mashed rutabagas. Roasts and steaks "rested" in the butter, and it glistened atop gravies. It enriched biscuits and cornbread and greased our lips magnificently.

At the base and to the right of the porch steps was the home of a pet crow. A flying accident had landed him at the bottom of the steps, knocked out and with a shattered wing. Perhaps the result of flight from a hungry hawk. Tender-hearted Jack erected a wooden-backed, screened-front cage on three-foot legs. There, Mr. Crow danced up and down his roost pole whistling and gazing skyward, first with one eye, and then the other, looking for imminent rescue by his kin that never came. I took a little stick and poked him in the breast so he would talk: "Craw, craw, mean ole craw." That's how it sounded as he wagged his head and danced. If he had a bit more cognition, he might have pronounced, "Child, child, mean ole child."

Mr. Crow was still alive, whistling and gazing at the sky, when I was offered a slot at Mama Haywood's Nursery School in town. I think my mother thought it was time for me to socialize with other children. I thought I should remain with Jack and Vasey. I cried bitterly, and Vasey cried too. After I started going to Mama Haywood's, I still stayed with Jack and Vasey every Friday, and our good times continued. Mama told Daddy she simply could not entirely part the three of us until first grade, which is another story.

People often reminisce about their early childhood years, and I assert that is true. I remember every one of mine in exquisite and loving detail. The world would be a better place if every child had a Jack and Vasey.

RABBIT

I moved about six years ago, and a lifetime of memories came spilling out of boxes untouched for decades. You know how that is—you accumulate, and you pile up, and you tuck away. Anyway, from a soiled and bedraggled stuffed fellow came this little bit of fluff in a story.

Rabbit lived with Father and Mother and Child on the corner of Trinity Chapel and Old Haw Creek Roads. He was a reassuring mix of soft navies, rusts, and browns—some plain and some patterned. He was thriftily stitched together from Father's old flannel gardening shirts, worn cotton bedsheets, and aprons that could not be mended one more time. The insides of his ears were vividly lined with the provocative pink of Mother's flowered silk slip torn one evening during playtime with Father.

He was not beautiful or fashionable as rabbits go. His physique was rather lumpy, the result of soft cotton batting stuffing. But he had the intrepid heart of an explorer, and Child loved him. When no one was looking, his droopy brown tapestry thread whiskers twitched with curiosity, and his black button eyes gleamed with lively expectation of adventure.

Rabbit was worn from numerous trips to town and being held tightly in Child's perspiring hands in church, and torn from exploration in the wider world. He proudly wore splotches of breakfast oatmeal and splatterings of fruit juice and hot chocolate. Child potted him into Mother's philodendron, and on more than one occasion, he swam in the toilet and in the soapy tub.

Rabbit was guest of honor at Child's tea parties and had a front row seat at the Plaza Theatre's Saturday matinees. He favored Walt Disney's "Fantasia." He was a bit curious though, for he had never seen Mother's broom dance like it did in the movie.

He assisted Child in excavating for red worms and roly-polys in the back yard and sometimes spent warm summer nights tucked into the stacked rock wall that enclosed the garden. There, he communicated with passing owls who circled him curiously, friendly little striped garter snakes, and magical golden orb weaver spiders that seemed to have knowledge written in their webs. It has been said that animals discern each other's thoughts. Rabbit had many friends in the natural world.

All in all, he was a well-traveled fellow, and should have been satisfied. But he longed for extended journeys on his own itinerary.

Then there was the day Father brought home the shiny, red pedal fire engine. Child heretofore in the custody of Father and Mother, got a taste of independent motion. Rabbit found himself in the less desirable environment of the toy box. There he languished over the summer, fussing at confinement and itchy for adventure. "Oh dear, life is passing me by," he thought as he heard Child cranking around the corner of the house in the red pedal fire engine.

Child was at nursery school the morning Mother felt cold-hearted enough to sort the toy box. One pile for the Salvation Army, one set aside for sentiment, and one for the trash bin. Her appraising eye and hand lingered over the soiled and tattered rabbit, but sanitation won and out to the curb he went. (You remember I said Mother was in a cold-hearted mood.) His round black eyes glinted in the sun, and one leg flopped over the side of the can. He smelled the great outdoors, heard birdsong both nearby and far off, and he felt his bond to Child loosening.

"What shall I see now, and where shall I go?" He rolled one eye around for possibilities. "I just know that great adventures are on the way!"

Rabbit looked behind him and spied a big black Labrador retriever taking in the enticing smells of each can just ahead of the lumbering, diesel-fuming garbage truck. Dog approached sniffing curiously.

"Oho, transportation! Let's go see the world," Rabbit squeaked, referencing the smelly truck drawing quite near.

"Oh, no! You know not of the horrors of the land-fill, Rabbit. I've been there—you don't want to go."

"Then help me out of this can—please do!"

Dog jumped up on his hind legs and retrieved Rabbit with a soft mouth. They set off on a gentle canter down Trinity Chapel. Dog gamboling lazily along, Rabbit flopping. What a perspective he had up high in Dog's mouth! His heart expanded with the smells of warm grass and dandelions. A bouquet of flower scents in roadside perennial borders and the raw watery smell of maturing sweet corn enticed his twitching nose. "Ooooh, I'm free!" he trilled. His attention was soon drawn by a confusing duality of aromas wafting down through the tree limbs and plumping up from the hot asphalt. The slight breeze ruffled his silken ears and tickled his whiskers. Deep purple star-shaped clematis and pink and blue crepe morning glories raced Dog and Rabbit along the tops of fence rows, and the spiky, tall hollyhocks bent their necks in greeting.

"Oh, thank you my friend," Rabbit whispered to Dog.

Dog almost dropped him when he stopped to growl at a porch cat, but Rabbit didn't mind. He was thrilling to his independence.

However . . .

On the next block they crossed paths with Mother walking Child home from nursery school. They were deep in conversation about the nursery lunch when Child looked over. "Look, look! That Dog has Rabbit!" Child began to gasp and cry.

It dawned on Mother in a flash that tragedy, emotional trauma, and future relational difficulties with her only child were imminent. She hitched her skirt up above her knees and took off after Dog, leaving Child whimpering on the sidewalk with a stern admonishment, "Don't you move until I get back."

Dog picked up his pace and began to run.

"Ouch! Ouch!" squeaked Rabbit as Dog's jaws tightened around him in the effort of escape. "Ow! Ow!" It was not so much fun now, being crushed in the mouth of Dog. "Ow, ow, oh-oh, please put me down!"

Dog, seeing Mother was gaining on him and swinging her purse over her head, obligingly dropped Rabbit into a soft flowerbed. "Bye-bye little fella—have a good life."

Dog ran off barking gaily as Mother fetched up panting, daubing at her face with a lace hanky drawn from her bosom. Her flowered rayon dress clung wetly to her back and thighs and her gait was offset by a broken heel. "Ach!" She was disgusted with the saliva-dripping, torn Rabbit, but nevertheless, she scooped him up and returned him with guilty resignation to Child's eagerly grasping hands.

Gulping through tears and a runny nose, Child asked, "But why did Rabbit want to leave home?"

Mother knelt down into the dirt and embraced Child and Rabbit. "Darling, that story can wait until you are older and love me more."

And so Rabbit came home, his traveling spirit now confined to the tax-paid property. But care and safety made up for wild adventures. Tucked into the red pedal fire engine against Child's warm side, *crank, crank,* he found pleasure and security in domestic routine and lived out his life in the company of Father and Mother and Child.

PROJECT MANAGEMENT

Have you ever looked back and thought how your childhood play and early interests informed your career paths, your direction and quality of life? Where are you now in your goals, set and met? I began to practice my avocation of project management early on. At age six, in fact.

If you are a product of single child-ness, you are always looking for something to come alongside, to entertain you, to be your partner. For me, it was my father's Florsheim shoebox stuffed with crayons from the 128-count Crayola Big Box. In addition, dozens of colored pencils and tiny wooden sharpeners with bitsy razor blades inside. I carried them with me everywhere so I would be ready for my next artistic project.

At three o'clock, the lower forms of St. Genevieve's Academy for Girls lined up in the large assembly room. The nuns inspected us for clean hands and faces, neat clothing, and tidy hair, so our mothers would gladly welcome us home. At the exact moment we were signaled to board St. Gen's blue bus, my tiny hands inevitably lost their grip on the shoebox, sending its contents merrily rolling under foot into the far corners of the room. The orderly lines of little girls broke ranks as all dashed after the runaways, book bags flung down and hair flying.

Mother Superior tolerated this noisy affront to order for the first four days of the school year. On Friday, she sent home a note, the first of many notes and phone calls that began with, "Dr. Serota, I have little Catherine in my office. Can you come?" After the third note was sent home, "little" was dropped from my name. Serendipitous art projects were now confined to weekends at home. I hoped I would manage the next project better.

At eight years of age, the second project began in a little patch of woods adjacent to three properties in East Asheville. Our house was situated on an acre lot in the curve of Hampden Road. On one side lived a family with two girls, and on the other, parents with a single girl. Upland from our homes lay a ten-acre tract of dense, beautiful woods. It belonged to an elderly widow who had no children and was delighted to have the four of us girls to watch at play. We each chose an area of the woods in which to build our playhouses. We swept the ground to bare dirt and created walls from sticks woven into rough wattle-style fences stuffed with leaves and twigs. Older boys came up from Canterbury Road to hassle us. We defended our territory with cudgels and sharp white oak acorns launched from slingshots crafted by Beth's father. The boys did not attempt to assault our holdings again. The widow cheered us from her back porch down below.

My three friends' floorplans had kitchens where they cooked up mud confections in their mothers' pots and dishes they toted to the woods every morning. Around four-thirty, their mothers appeared in the woods to retrieve their dishes and start supper. Their playhouses also had nurseries for their doll babies, made cozy with toys, blankets, cradles, and strollers. Every morning and evening a procession of household articles and personal possessions made its way to and from the woods.

My house was a bit different. It had a chapel. Mother's stately sterling candlesticks fitted with blue tapers sat upon a cardboard box draped with her white Irish linen tablecloth "borrowed" from the china cabinet drawer. There was also a filched silver crucifix my father had carried through World War II and my small leather New Testament. My goal was to interest my friends in morning devotions like I had at St. Genevieve's. I offered a quasi-Catholic worship service featuring solemn Latin intonations, a short homily, and a Baptist-style communion of grape juice and saltine crackers. Oh, and Bible verse memorization too.

The three looked at each other, snickered, and begged off. "Nooooo—We're not kneeling down in the dirt. Too many rocks."

That was disappointing, as I reflected on the state of their immortal souls.

Next, I tried to usher them into the classroom. I had laid boards over cinder blocks for seating and carried up my chalkboard easel. Each night I devised a lesson plan complete with written exercises and a pop quiz of multiple choice and fill-in-the-blank questions. My teaching modules included world geography, the three branches of the American government, and ancient history. I wanted to share my love of learning.

This time they laughed out loud and wrinkled up their noses, "Ancient history? We don't have that at Haw Creek. Besides, this is summertime and we're not going to school!"

I even offered to exempt them from the written essay questions. They were not interested. What went wrong? My best marketing strategies had failed. I produced three report cards and gave the rating of "Unsatisfactory" for their attitudes. They returned to raising their doll babies and creating clouds of dust "cleaning" in their mothers' best dinner party aprons.

"Anne Catherine Serota!" An angry shout from down below. My mother had not been able to find the candlesticks and tablecloth for the Ladies Circle meeting she was organizing. Unfazed, I packed up the chapel and the school room, dragged the boards and cinderblocks downhill to the back of the garage. I holed up in my room with my Siamese cat and a pad of paper.

Enter project number three.

I was inspired by the possibilities of the woodland playhouses. I would design and build a real, kind of, community on paper and call it "Clear Creek Township." My father was in the school supply business, and I could pillage the Aladdin's Cave of Morgan Brothers School Supply any time I wanted. I considered myself now in the development business, armed with graph paper and onionskin tracing sheets. A T-square, protractor, compass, ruler, and an assortment of pens, pencils, and erasers rounded out my tool kit. My supportive parents gifted me with a junior drafting table.

Soon, floor plans and elevations, complete with rights of way for streets, parking lots, and infrastructure, poured off the little drafting table. I created schools, offices, homes, a community center and a park with a lake. I worked long after my parents had gone to bed, a rolled-up towel stuffed against the base of my door to hide the lamplight. It was summer and I could sleep in a little. Another month, and another school year began.

My father took me to the Buncombe County Tax Records Office, where I looked at plats and property taxes in different parts of the county and decided where to locate Clear Creek Township. We then visited W.H. Westall's lumber yard and supply company. I calculated estimates for lumber, concrete, block, brick, roofing, and interiors. I arrived at costs per square foot after many hours of hard calculating and complex figuring. A huge piece of cardboard laid out on the living room floor became the township boundaries and I moved the plan pieces around on it like a big-shot developer. This was so exciting! Finally, I wrote advertising facsimile for *The Asheville Citizen-Times* and fliers for an open house.

Two years after I began, I pitched the design to my parents. They selected a floor plan and reserved a choice lot across from the park. I was six years away from college admission, but I requested the School of Architecture catalogue from North Carolina State in Raleigh.

Enter Aunt Winona when I turned eleven. She sent me a folio of large, beautiful twelve-inch paper dolls. They arrived in the mail from Texas and sported an eye-popping array of all-occasion outfits—even an English riding kit. This, she told my mother, was her effort to "civilize and lady-fy little Anne Catherine." She was certain I was growing up to be a barbarian.

I was certain I was plenty "lady-fied." I examined the gift and decided I could design my own creations for the dolls. Putting the school supplies and drafting table to good use, I replicated an early-1960s closetful of clothing and accessories for a fashionable teenager—a twelve inch one, that is. Mother relayed my pleasure in her gift to Aunt Winona, who traveled from Fort Worth for a visit.

Aunt Winona was Mother's older sister and believed herself to be the better of the whole family, having bettered herself through three marriages to increasingly wealthy men. I could not fathom why any man would want to marry Aunt Winona. She was over six feet tall, churlish, and overbearing, with a hatchet face capable of sending a bear squalling into the mountains. Daddy said if a western diamondback rattler bit her, the poor snake would die. I was not fond of her visits for she bullied my mother, criticized my every move and statement, and mercilessly compared me unfavorably to her husband's golden niece, Amanda.

Aunt Winona made an ugly little moue at the paper doll wardrobe and sniffed at the mock-up of Clear Creek Township. I boiled inwardly and stuck my tongue out at her back. Mother shook her finger and her head and smiled. I had to give up my bed to her and sleep on sofa cushions on the living room floor. I didn't even have the solace of my Siamese. The cat was boarded with a neighbor because Aunt Winona was mortally terrified of scratches and bites and was sure my cat was a vicious killer. I could have told her Nana wouldn't bite her—she preferred to live. Life was simply not good when Aunt Winona was in town.

It was the week before Easter, and Aunt Winona wanted to display her largesse by purchasing a pair of lady-like white gloves to go with my Easter outfit. The plan was to shop at Ivey's in town, then return straightaway home for Mother's luscious pot roast dinner. Mother loaned Aunt Winona her car for the trip, and I obligingly directed the way downtown. The gloves were bought, Coca-Colas were drunk at Woolworth's lunch counter, and we returned to the car.

Ha! She was in my power now. I had total control over the trip home and I was going to make it memorable! I directed her up Patton Avenue to Pack Square and right down Biltmore Avenue into the Village. We drove up and down the cobblestone and brick streets while I pointed out the shops and All Souls Church, the fruit of George Vanderbilt's design.

"Well, that's nice, but I'm getting hungry!" she snapped.

I nodded and we drove around Amboy Road over the Swannanoa River to the back gate of the Biltmore Estate. The porter recognized me as Mother often consulted on horticulture projects there, and he waved us through. We tooled along the two-mile drive to the house and conservatory, back down by the river fields, and fetched up at the dairy barn. I saw many of my friends playing there, and we waved to each other. They were the children of the employees who lived and worked at the estate.

I asked Aunt Winona to stop. "Certainly not, they are dirty ruffians! Why is your mother allowing you to consort with farm children? Take me home—it's getting late."

"Certainly," I said, waving goodbye to my friends and smiling to myself.

We left Biltmore, and instead of turning right on Swannanoa River Road toward home, I directed her left toward the Asheville freight depot down on the French Broad River. It was a dirty and smelly place with rotting offal heaped up outside a nearby slaughterhouse and noxious fumes from several factory smokestacks. Hovels carpeted the slopes behind the river. Drunken men were lounging about unpainted shacks that discreetly sold liquor out the back doors after dark. The river chugged by, swollen with debris and orange mud from storm run-off.

Aunt Winona began to gag and she rubbed her irritated eyes. Presently, tears began to seep out. Her voice rose. "Why are we here? This is horrible! There are cutthroats and criminals everywhere, and those horrid-looking women—slatterns and prostitutes! This is not the way home!"

Wide-eyed and innocent, I responded in my best surprised voice. "Why, Auntie, I thought you would enjoy seeing where Daddy comes to unload boxcars with the boys."

"The boys? What boys? Unload boxcars? Down here in this filth?" Her voice was now shrilling above high C, and there was a most satisfying look of horror and disbelief on her face.

Miss Innocence answered. "Well of course Mama knows he does it to keep fit and to keep an eye on the boys from work—it's all right. Daddy could fight his way out of here if he had to—he knows jujitsu!"

"Fight?" One last cough and gasp and she collapsed back against the seat, wiping her eyes. "Catherine, if you do not direct me out of this place at once . . ." And with a retching gasp, words failed her.

Really—she was finally quiet.

I set sail for Lyman Street and a few miles hence, turned up Broadway, Chestnut, and into the Montford neighborhood. Left on Pearson Drive and I pointed out where I had spent happy childhood days at Mama Haywood's Nursery School.

Aunt Winona recovered the power of speech. "Your mother left you here?"

"Oh yes, it was fine. I loved Mama Haywood, and we never saw Daddy Haywood until he had slept off his drunk after lunch."

"What? Drunk?" She was getting tuned up again. "I have some things to say to your mother. Boxcars, drunks—I, I never heard of such things, and common laborers' children for playmates? I . . . I . . .," she stuttered.

The last stop on the tour of Asheville's finer sights was one block over—the Riverside Cemetery. We rolled in through the gates and came to an abrupt stop.

"I have had enough, Anne Catherine. If your mother doesn't discipline you when we get home, I will!"

"Why, Aunt Winona, this is a famous place! O'Henry and Thomas Wolfe are buried here, and Zelda Fitzgerald burned up at the Highland Hospital just over there. I'll show you . . . come . . ."

"You are a heathen and completely undeserving of human kindness!" she screamed. Rolling down the car window, she grabbed the Ivey's bag from the backseat and flung it out. The bag floated down upon the grave of a little girl, dead in the 1918 flu epidemic, and the gloves slapped the hovering marble angel squarely in the face. "So there!" she bellowed.

I tasted victory, hugged myself in delight, and managed to exhibit faux-humility on the—at last—trip home.

Aunt Winona roared into the house, ranting at Mother and Daddy as she packed up. She called a cab and waited at the curb for it, without the roast beef supper, and left straightway for the airport and Texas with her wounded dignity. She never returned.

I regained my bed that evening and was only slightly punished by being denied dessert. I cuddled with the Siamese cat. I heard Mother and Daddy laughing far into the night before I dropped off to sleep. I truly felt I had managed this project masterfully.

There is one concept learned in my younger years that has informed my life's path: Careful planning, organization, and perseverance are essential elements in project management.

THE AWFULEST CHRISTMAS TREE

The year I was five years old, Mama, Daddy, and I moved from Haw Creek across the highway and built a house. My mother, who was a botanist, loved all growing things and had a thumb green up to her shoulder. Our lot had been cleared of all trees except for one towering red oak. She determined to populate our acre with multi-purpose conifers—live Christmas trees that were beautifully decorated, lit, and displayed in the living room picture window, then planted outside to thrive in the yard. The spruce of the year was tagged early in November out at Jesse Israel's nursery in Candler. Mama and I always enjoyed this outing. She would walk through the fields with Jesse, discussing new plants and old favorites, then we would have lunch at the Biltmore Dairy Bar on the way home. There was always the fresh, creamy Biltmore ice cream for dessert, made right there on the estate. On the Saturday after Thanksgiving, Daddy and I drove back out to Israel's in the big Ford truck and brought back the 100-pound balled and burlapped spruce. On the way back, he and I stopped at Buck's Drive-in. That was his favorite.

While we were gone, Mama baked Christmas goodies: sugar cookies in wondrous shapes decorated with colorful icing, sprinkles, and silver shot, chocolate fudge with nuts, fruitcake, and walnut divinity. This was a day's worth of love involving billows of flour, confectioner's sugar, boiling substances, a candy thermometer, and almost every bowl, pot, implement, and utensil in the kitchen. In Mama's mind, the live tree, the Christmas goodies, the Asheville Parade, and Handel's *Messiah* defined our family's Christmas tradition, and she loved and defended it.

The year I was nine years old, Mama announced she was planting the final conifer. Not the Serbian, Colorado blue, Engelman, or Norway spruce of former years, but the crown regent of Christmas trees—the Fraser fir. Full and lush with dark emerald, velvety-soft needles and that sticky green resinous Christmas smell—the perfect tree!

Mama said to Daddy, "John, will you select our Christmas tree this year?" She wrote down the perfect tree's specifications: six to seven feet with a proper correlation of terminal to skirt. "Just make sure Jesse sells you a premium tree." She handed the paper to Daddy, who smiled and folded it into his wallet.

The next afternoon we drove downtown to the parade. It formed up on Valley Street behind the police and fire departments, wrapped around Pack Square, marched down Patton Avenue, executed a sharp right turn at Pritchard Park, and swept smartly up Haywood Street. There were convertibles sponsored by civic organizations with beauty queens shivering in their pageant gowns. Fire trucks from every community in Western North Carolina blaring and squelching their sirens. High school bands from the seven surrounding counties proudly strutting. Horse riders wearing cowboy outfits, clowns and jugglers capering about, and acrobats flipping all over the street. So many floats— some with seasonal tableaux and others advertising local businesses.

We craned our necks to see the Stevens Lee High School High-Steppers beating out a tantalizing tattoo on their drum line, their majorettes sweeping the street from side to side as they tossed and caught flaming batons. Hard candies and pennies were thrown from floats into the crowds lining the sidewalks The excitement of the opening season, the lights, the decorated shop windows with their embellishments of red, green, and gold, and the resonance of the bands' percussion sections pounded in my chest and made me pant with excitement. I barely had breath to holler "Hey Santa!" when he appeared. Oh, it was hard to go to sleep that night as "Old King Cole was a merry old soul" replayed in my head.

My father was up early the next morning making breakfast. He had already pulled boxes of outside lights and decorations from the attic and set them in the front yard. He handed me a twenty-dollar bill with a wink and whispered, "After you help Mama with the goodies and go uptown, you get her a nice present. There will be a real surprise waiting for you when you get back."

Oh boy, I thought, *the tree will be up, and we can decorate it.*

Mama and I made red-and-white-striped candy cane cookies, chocolate pecan fudge, and the lightest, most delicious walnut divinity ever! We drove to town and visited Ivey's, John Carroll, and Bon Marche, where my twenty dollars purchased a stately-sculpted bottle of Charles of the Ritz hand lotion (my father called it "Charles of the Snoots"). Mama pretended to browse the glove counter while my purchase was wrapped. The store was alive with eager shoppers, fantasy displays, perfumed air, and mannequins dressed in sumptuous furs and finery. Strings of pearls and evergreen garlands sparkling with fairy lights festooned the corners of the store and met in a huge crush of multi-colored glass balls in the center of the store. Mama reminded me, "Ladies don't gape," as I whirled and twirled around to capture all the sights.

One of the outside windows had been turned into a fantasy forest with child-sized brown velvet teddy bears dressed in red vests, white Peter Pan collars, and black patent leather boots. They were kicking and bowing to "It's Beginning to Look a Lot Like Christmas." Children's faces were plastered to the glass as they gazed in wonder at the mechanized bears. "Come along. come along, now," said their mothers, pulling them away.

At The Man Store on Patton Avenue, Mama purchased Daddy a new camel hair overcoat, and I selected a brown and tan silk tie with HER twenty-dollar bill.

Our eyes were shining with our gifts, the goodies at home, and the promise of a beautiful tree in the window. What a Christmas it would be, with Santa yet to come! Armed with the presents and take-out from Buck's Drive in, we danced in through the kitchen and tapped at the French doors.

"Jo-ohn, may we come in-n-n?" trilled Mama. She looked at me and we both wriggled with delight and expectation.

"Just a minute, I'm turning on the lights." Then the doors sprang open to my father's smiling face. "Come in my dears and see your Christmas tree!"

Mama and I stepped into the living room and suddenly, with one great *whoosh*, Mama sucked all the oxygen out of the room. Oh no! Where were the soft bouncy limbs? The glowing lights? The hand-blown German glass ornaments? The red-feathered cardinals and the gold and crimson bows? Where were the huge glass globes whose surfaces contained the whole room? And the presiding delicate, lacy china angel? Where were they?

A spinning wheel of garish primary colors illuminated this . . . this prickly aberration atop the drum table in the window. Perched upon Mama's hand-embroidered tree skirt sat a four-foot aluminum pole in a stand with sixteen naked metal branches tipped with exploded tinsel rosettes. Tiny plastic balls dangled dismally from each branch. The wheel squeaked in time to the stereo playing, "Oh Christmas tree—*wreenk*—Oh Christmas tree—*wreenk*—how lovely are your—*wreenk*—branches."

It was the awfullest Christmas tree ever!

Mama blinked, swallowed hard, and croaked, "Oh, John—what is it? It's . . . it's . . . it's . . . not real."

Giving Daddy a thin smile, she turned, tilted, and cruised into the kitchen, touching base with every door facing and piece of furniture in her path. Sinking into a chair at the table, she uttered a series of cries that my father later described, discreetly, as "A dying calf in a hailstorm under a tin roof." With a flourish of her wrist, she sent the platter of divinity in a graceful four-foot arc—*crash!*—into the trash can. As the china made a two-point landing, my startled Siamese cat pirouetted up from her basket, careened around the corner into the living room, and crashed into the color wheel, before scrambling, her tail bottle-brushed, for parts unknown in the back of the house. The color wheel, mortally wounded and laying on its side, was sawing and hawing to the unctuous strains of "O Holy Night"—*uurh*.

The year I was thirty-six years old, Mama, Daddy, and I sat on the front porch of the log house I built in Haywood County. Spread out before us, shimmering in the late October sunlight and bristling with buyers' flagging, were two of the twenty-one acres of Fraser fir I would eventually set on our land.

Pointing to a stately eight-foot beauty, Mama said, with just a little attitude, "Look, John, THAT is a real Christmas tree."

And she never let him forget it.

ADVENTURES IN FLORA AND FAUNA

My mother, Cornelia Ann Roach Serota, strode purposefully through the male-dominated world of collegiate physical sciences during the 1940s, '50s, '60s, and '70's with all the grace inherent in a southern lady. When she retired in 1976, she was a twenty-five-year research associate of the National Science Foundation. The foundation is a federally funded grantor of monies for the exploration and furtherance of American scientific endeavors. She was also an associate professor of botany. Her field was genetics, and she became an international authority on the trillium, a wildflower indigenous to several forested areas of the world, including the southern Appalachians. She was completing her doctorate as I was completing my schooling at St. Genevieve of the Pines Academy in Asheville.

I was her favorite field research assistant. The federal and several state governments had provided her with collecting permits. We visited her research plots in parks, national forests, and wilderness areas up and down the Appalachians. But our favorite was Great

Smoky Mountains National Park, whose diverse elevations and exposures held every variety of trillium in
the country. I say "our" favorite because she occasion-
ally absented me from St. Gens to accompany her so I
could learn and share her knowledge of the forest won-
ders. The park could easily be circumnavigated in a
day, which was an additional bonus. It was not entirely
a play day away from school for me, however; Mother
Latour in the botany lab required me to submit a paper
on what I had seen and learned during my absence.

One pristine day in very early April 1963, we were
working in a plot off Highway 441, about six miles east
of Gatlinburg, Tennessee. The weather was warm and
sunny. Early plants were emerging, including showy
orchis, bloodroot, and trilliums. We were digging in
an area about half a mile from the road when our
ears pricked up. We were accustomed to the noises
of the forest: bird song, a deer crashing through the
undergrowth and snorting at our presence, the warning rattle of a nearby viper, the roar of a creek swollen
by rain, the sound of rain itself splashing through the
canopy down the slopes toward us. But on this day, we
were startled by a far-off sound of tussle and rumpus.

It originated on a high ridge of the area named
The Chimneys, a dense and sticky rhododendron hell
peppered with tall hemlock and hickory. It was coming
closer, and we soon heard slashing sounds through the
trees and strange high-pitched yelps and low growls.

We stood still as our hearts began to beat wildly in our chests. No fight or flight response, just pure freeze. The tumult drew closer; some creature was bawling and snapping its jaws. The approach was so rapid we had no time to run to the car a couple thousand feet away, even if we could have moved our feet. I was certain this was my last trip, my last day alive. Mother's arm swung out and swept me behind her. I peeped around her waist—I had to see what was about to happen. A yearling black bear with wide brown eyes in a sea of startled white crashed out of the understory and charged us. A horrible oily rankness preceded the bear. Just as Mother raised her arms to shield us, it barreled past and with one more loud bawl, plunged into the laurel behind us. Mother spun around and we exchanged open-mouthed gapes. Our tongues were too dry to speak.

BUT THAT WAS NOT ALL!

In a flash we saw the reason for the young bear's panicked flight. Out from the thicket exploded a large, yellow-eyed, male bobcat, its brindled fur on edge. Paws and claws scrambled for a hold in the gravely dirt with the objective of dinner on its broad bewhiskered face. In another blink of the eye, it was also gone, growling as it sprang past us into the undergrowth. Could there possibly be more to this desperate chase? The loudest, smelliest, and most dangerous beast was yet to come. Emerging with an immense roar from the thicket was the infuriated mother of the yearling. She was huge and beautiful and well-fed for just two months out of brumation, with thick brownish-black fur rippling in the sun. Her mouth was open, gasping for air, and we were shocked by her sharp, saliva-dripping, yellow teeth. Her five-inch claws dug furrows in the earth, and her body shook with fury and the effort of pursuit. I squealed. I couldn't help myself. The bear briefly swung her massive head in my direction and made eye contact, but there was no hesitation in her pursuit of the cat and her offspring. She swept past in a cloud of malodorous musk. We never saw her latest cub, born over the winter. It was probably hustled up into a hemlock for safety.

Mother and I stood still, listening as the tussle and rumpus disappeared over the ridge behind us. We collapsed into the dirt laughing and sobbing our relief, allowing the terror hormones to seep from our bodies. Collecting trillium was forgotten that day. We drove, still trembling, into Gatlinburg and enjoyed a lavish survivors' supper.

Mother Latour was impressed with the paper I submitted entitled, "Adventures with Flora and Fauna." She read it to the class. They were impressed by my tale of surviving one bobcat and two bear "attacks," as I embellished them just a bit.

Mother and I enjoyed many more field trips, and we never again experienced one with such great adrenalin-enhanced adventure.

BISCUITS

When I was first married to Bob in 1982, I knew nothing about making biscuits. We were busy people in my childhood house and we had toast. It was quick and easy. So here I am, a Southern Appalachian first-time bride of thirty-two, married to a mountain man from Madison County, and I have no bread-making skills. Bob's first wife, Marilyn, was a famous baker, which put my back up to begin with. So on the Wednesday of our third week of marriage, I decided to make biscuits. I began with flour and baking powder and baking soda. Because I'm baking, right? I added a couple of tablespoons of salt and a lump of shortening and some milk. A stick of butter and an egg rounded it out. I stirred and stirred and stirred, but the butter would not incorporate; it refused to melt. I put the bowl in the microwave and zapped it for five minutes on high. Well, it all boiled up and over and there were two messes to clean up. I scraped what I could back into the bowl.

It looked a bit strange.

I liberally floured the counter and turned the dough out into the flour. I had to scrape and scrape to get the mess out of the bowl. It took a lot of flour to get the stickiness out—A LOT of flour. In fact, I had flour all over me, the counter, and the floor. Flour hung in the air and gently sifted down onto every kitchen surface. The mass of dough didn't look quite right to me, but I had gone too far to quit now. When I got discouraged, I just visualized Marilyn's haughty expression and I got fresh perspective.

I remembered I had received a rolling pin as a wedding present from someone who thought I had domestic skills. I took it out of the drawer and floured it, having a faint memory of my mother doing that. I looked down at the counter—the dough was quite an impressive lump. Heavy and willing to defy the rolling pin. I tried to roll the mass out but I only rolled it up onto the pin where it stuck—fast.

"Okay," I huffed.

My next brilliant idea was to take a butcher knife and cut the dough off the pin. It was hard work scraping the recalcitrant dough off the surface of the rolling pin, and it took forever.

Great! Now there were wood splinters in my biscuits. I cut the last of the mass off, and it fell heavily down onto the floured counter. *THUMP!* More flour rose into the air. I rolled it around, punched it a bit, and danced a few steps as I hummed the Rocky theme, picking at the splinters in my palms. I pinched off chunks, rolled them between my hands, "Ooh, ow!" and flattened them to make patties, incorporating more splinters. They now looked like baby porcupines. I knew they went into the oven, but how hot? Remembering Mama said pot roast should cook long and slow, I figured that would do for biscuits too, so I turned the oven to 300 degrees and slid the cookie sheet in. I was feeling better about it all. Now we would have some biscuits!

Forty-five minutes later they were just sitting there. I thought they would have risen like they were supposed to—light and fluffy. But no, there they sat in their lump-like state. I swear I saw Marilyn's face grinning archly up at me.

"Okay, Marilyn, I'll just fire you up!" I said with a vengeance. I turned on the broiler to brown them. They would look more appetizing, and so would she! I visited the bathroom and returned to find the biscuits seriously sunburned and blistered. The kitchen was filling with a horrid, smoky cloud. I dragged the cookie sheet and the ruined biscuits from the oven and set them atop the stove, burning my fingers. What to do now?

At that very moment, Bob walked in from work, waving his arms through the smoke, and over to the stove. He looked down at the biscuits; he looked at me. He picked one up. "OUCH!" It was hot, and he dropped it onto the floor where it bounced one, two, three times into the utility room. He was laughing so hard he staggered across the kitchen and collapsed into a chair. Between guffaws he gasped, "Why are you baking cow patties?" Tears streamed from his eyes and plopped into gummy flour puddles on the floor. Well, that was the final straw. My lower lip came out and I also dissolved in tears—not of laughter but of failure, shame, and the humiliating thought that he was probably wondering why he had given up Marilyn's fine cooking for this mess. I ran upstairs and, true to crying brides everywhere, flung myself across the bed sobbing heart-brokenly. Bob followed, attempting to console me. "Honey, don't cry, I married you for your mind! I can always eat loaf bread." Leaving me dramatically weeping, he returned downstairs, cleaned up the kitchen, and threw the "cow patties" to the dogs.

The final humiliation? The dogs didn't eat them either.

DUCK

Well, you've read my story about the biscuit debacle. But it appears I didn't learn. For later that year, in 1982, knowing my husband's love for crispy duck, I decided to surprise him with one. We had dined at the Chinese restaurant in Asheville the prior Friday evening and enjoyed their Peking duck with pancakes and sauce. It was truly a luscious dish. The pancakes so light with the lovely caramelized deep brown sauce. And the duck—tender inside with a crisp golden crust that crackled when you bit into it. So delicious. But I was tired of driving forty miles to the restaurant. Why not enjoy the dish at home? So I asked our server the method of preparation. He rolled his eyes back in his head; his laughter finally died down to a chuckle.

"Missy, that take many days for the duck and many thing you have to do," he choked out. "The cook," he said, gesturing toward the kitchen, "he has secret way to make."

"Well, you must have seen him make it. What did he do?" I was persistent.

The beset server mumbled something about dropping the duck into water with five spices and hanging it up to dry, then baking it, and finally searing it. My husband looked at me, and I knew he was remembering the biscuits two months before. I had not attempted them again. I screwed up my mouth and furrowed my brow at him. It was not a happy look at all, but it did not deter him for a minute.

"I don't think you ought to try this. I don't mind driving to Asheville for duck—I really don't mind. I want to remember duck as a pleasant experience." He smiled, rather sarcastically, I thought. Well, that did it. I smiled back sweetly and vowed to myself that I would make the most delicious crispy Peking duck he had ever tasted.

We went home and I waited a few days so he would forget about the ducky conversation. As soon as he left for work one morning, I went directly to Ingles Market and found a six-pound duck in the frozen food section. I took it home, but it was too long to fit into the little microwave to thaw, so I dunked it in a sink of hot water. About four hours later it thawed. I knew I had to hurry as the server had said it took several days to prepare, and I had five hours. I would need some shortcuts. I recollected the first step was steeping the duck in water and spices. I didn't know what spices to use, but I remembered something about a five-spice powder which, of course, I did not have. I decided to make my own five-spice powder. I pulled garlic salt, onion pow-der, whole cloves, red pepper flakes, and nutmeg out of the cabinet and dumped them into a stockpot of hot water with the duck. It didn't exactly smell right but I thought the sharp, spicy cloves gave it a nice touch. I then added two cups of soy sauce because soy sauce was Asian, and this was a Chinese dish. The boiling duck reposed in this bath for an hour. I removed the duck and, remembering the hanging step, trussed it up on a coat hanger and hung it out on the front porch to drip dry. Only it was not drying fast enough. I had pierced the skin of the duck with the coat hanger, and because it was hot from its bath, liquified fat was pouring forth onto the porch. I had to dry it quickly. I got my hair-dryer and set to work. Of course, more fat came out, and so did the neighbor ladies. There were middle-aged married couples on either side of our house, and the wives came out and started laughing.

"What in tarnation are you doing to that poor hen?" one asked between sobs of laughter.

"It's not a chicken," I said with all the dignity I could muster. "It's a duck, and I'm drying it out."

"A duck? You're drying it out? What for, what are you going to do with it?"

"I'm fixing a surprise dinner for my husband," I responded with a little attitude.

"Well," the woman on the other side said, "I'm sure it WILL be a surprise."

Wiping their eyes with their aprons and holding their sides, they went back in. I knew they were calling up the neighborhood and telling them what the new wife was doing now. I tossed my head. I didn't care. They had never prepared a gourmet meal in their lives!

The duck appeared to finally have reached a state of dryness and collapse. It had relinquished a third of its weight to my preparations. I took it inside, turned the oven on, and set it at 325 degrees. *It needs to cook long and slow,* I thought. *Oh yes, put something on it.* I thought of the savory brown sauce and again made do with what I had. I mixed Heinz 57 sauce with dark brown sugar, vinegar, onions, raisins, and, of course, another cup of soy sauce because it was a Chinese dish. I slathered the duck top to bottom with it, slid the duck into the oven, and pulled up a chair to watch it cook.

An hour later it did not appear to have progressed far beyond a state of raw, so I turned on the broiler and set the duck three inches under it. I was running out of time. The sauce began to bubble and pop, and more fat poured into the bottom of the pan. In a minute, the fat ignited. I opened the door and was greeted by a blast of smoke and flames. Grabbing a box of salt, I flung it in the direction of the fire. The salt thankfully smothered the flames, and I was able to take out the remains a few minutes later.

Oh, my poor duck. It was charred up one side and down the other, and I scraped it for a good half an hour. The clock told me Bob would be home soon, and there was one more step the server had described— not including making the pancakes—the duck had to be seared to develop that wonderful crispy skin. It looked pretty seared to me already, and I wasn't sure it had any skin left, but I gamely returned to the porch where the small hibachi grill sat on two bricks and I fired it up. The curtains at the windows of the houses on either side billowed and twitched, and I knew those two women were watching me again. I thought I heard muffled howls and snorts.

I burned the duck further on all four sides, smoking it liberally in the charcoal fire. It stank of lighter fluid as I had no time to wait for the coals to die down a bit. It had magically swelled up again and now resembled a blackened football. I was lifting it from the grill when Bob drove up. In an instant, looking at the charred corpse, he knew what I had done. He began to laugh. He sat down on the front steps and put his head between his knees. Periodically he lifted his head and looked at the duck balancing on a large fork in my hands, then laughed some more. There were choking sounds. This encouraged the two women to emerge from their houses and stagger, laughing, over into our front yard. They approached the porch and looked at the duck, looked at me, looked at Bob, and started up all over again. Three grown people laughing their behinds off. At me and at my duck.

Well, that was the end. I wheeled around to go into the house and the duck, or what there was left of the poor thing, slipped off the fork, bounced down the steps, then took flight. It came to rest against the mailbox. One of the women choked out, "Air mail!" and threw her apron up over her head. I went into the house and sat down on the sofa.

I had done my best. Biscuits and crispy duck.

Never again!

LIFE AT MILL POND FARM

I guess you could say it's in my blood. My parents came from farm people's stock: my mother from an unproductive, dry dirt farm in West Texas, under which a vast oil reservoir was discovered during World War II, and my father, whose family grew citrus on hundreds of acres in the Rio Grande River Valley.

Mill Pond Farm is much smaller: just seventy-eight acres in the mountains of East Tennessee. We are bound by forest on all sides. The Appalachian Trail crosses Street's Gap just up the state road on the Tennessee-North Carolina line. Our livestock is mainly wild, except for a nineteen-year-old cat who lives indoors. The farm is roamed by bears, deer, bobcats, coyotes, raccoons, possums, skunks, field mice, wood rats, squirrels, rabbits, snapping turtles in the pond, box turtles in the grass, Appalachian ruffed grouse, and over ten kinds of snakes. There are also thirty species of migratory and permanent resident birds. During the growing months, it is an embarrassing riot of green and creates its own storied adventures. Like the time

I watched two deer grazing nonchalantly over the upper slope behind the house, followed purposefully by a huge, red wolf about three minutes later. The wildlife officer stated there were no red wolves, no wolves of any kind, living in East Tennessee, but I locked gaze with his cold yellow eyes and I beg to differ.

We have watched a bear grow to maturity over the past five years. As a yearling, we first spied him scooting from the woods across the driveway into the white pine grove. He was such a cute little fellow! The second year, he climbed up on a pile of bagged soil amendments, vaulted over the eight-foot deer fence, and made for the composter in the back of the garden. He proceeded to dismantle it looking for a choice morsel, then lumbered over the back fence and off into the woods. The third year we were awakened at two-thirty in the morning by a crash out back. The alarms began to sound, lights came on, and we sprang up from bed. The bear had attacked a sparrow's nest built inside the on-demand water heater unit on the back wall. He tore the machine to bits then ranged along to the tall, glass back door, stood up, and left his calling card by pressing his paws and snout against it. Not so cute now.

On a July night he made a tuchus-shaped bed in the wild blackberry brambles beside the garage. He then lay back like a Roman emperor, feasting at leisure. The fourth summer, he came calling during midday. He attempted to climb the pole where the bluebird house is mounted. He left an invitation for any sow bears in the neighborhood by rubbing his anal glands against two eight-foot specimen conifers in the yard, breaking them. They had to be cut down.

This past year, I found him on the bottom step of the deck, preparing to climb up to the bird feeders. I screamed and he ran off across the yard, back and forth, trying to find a passage through the fence. After attempting to climb it with his bulky self, he simply crushed it, somersaulted over onto his back, looked at me from the other side, and shuffled through the weeds into the woods. He is now a mature two-hundred-and-fifty to three-hundred-pound bear, glossy black and confident. He's not swayed by me standing on the deck screaming at him and beating on a pot with a ladle.

I ordered bear spray from Amazon. I read the label. The chemicals are more dangerous for me than the bear! I am instructed to go immediately to the emergency room if I discharge the spray, and there are no guarantees that it will deter the bear from making me dinner.

I mentioned the eight-foot fence. We built the garden frames and I planted them before the house was even built. That first year was a disaster. Every deer and their cousin fed liberally off my efforts; the Shealy Buffet. We started off with a black plastic mesh fence displayed in the slick gardeners' catalogue. The advertisement guaranteed the fence would scare off the deer when they touched it. Allegedly, they cannot see it in the dark and would be spooked when their noses made contact. But, of course, deer can see in the dark! We erected the mesh around the garden area. The deer were unsure at first and shied away. Then one brave individual put her head through it, then her sharp hoofs.

The fence was systematically shredded, and the deer came and went in the garden. I initially attempted to mend it, stitching the torn places together with yarn. The whole fence became a modern work of art covered with spider webs. That didn't work; the deer simply made new holes. Our pair of eastern phoebes, gray rat snakes, and colubar constrictors known as black snakes became enmeshed. I cut them all loose with scissors. The poor Phoebes died from shock. The snakes were unhappy at being handled and tried to bite. Finally, my husband found metal fencing at the farmer's co-op. It was purchased for a local zoo that didn't take it. We did. Deer will jump a six-foot fence but not an eight-foot fence, unless they are in flight for their lives. We also enclosed the entire front of the house's landscaped slope. Our property resembled a prison exercise yard. The deer were locked out. But the rabbits, whistle pigs, and possums could come through.

The garden is important. I grow many plants from seed in the greenhouse and set them into frames four-foot by sixteen-foot long. We freeze and can the produce. There are also hybrid raspberry and blackberry vines on trellises, strawberries, and blueberries. On occasion, fruit plants have to be replaced, such as the winter when the temperature plunged to negative four degrees. I am questioning the wisdom of growing and weeding strawberry frames for the purpose of feeding birds. The berries bloom heavily and set thousands of fruits, but I picked perhaps one hundred pock-free berries last spring.

We admire our long greasy beans. A true heirloom bean, they have history and a pedigree, developed by my mother some forty years ago. They are a major part of our winter diet. In 2021, the year Covid afflicted the country so terribly, my husband flew to a business conference in Chicago on August 19. I could not go because we were in the middle of the garden harvest and I was picking and canning beans and tomatoes every three days.

The morning he left, I developed what I assessed as a garden-variety sinus infection; I had had them frequently in the past and it was no big deal. By that night, the infection had morphed into what turned out to be a horrible battle with Covid. I stayed awake all night. My temperature flared at 103 degrees, then I shivered with chills. I could not breathe and felt the coughing was breaking my bones apart. I truly believed I was dying. My frantic husband could not rent a car or fly back as he had told the airways personnel I had Covid and was home alone. He had to have a swab test and be negative for three days.

During this interim, thieves crept past our gate, up our road, and cut two frames of beans loose from the vines. Bushels of Long Greasy Beans were selling for $130 in the local farmers' markets, and three bushels were stolen. Several days later the sheriff told us that five farms in the Flag Pond community had lost beans. The culprits were never found. The garden gate is now locked, there is a camera, and I check those beans several times a day.

But there are beauty spots—oh, so many beautiful moments. Last week, the full June Strawberry Moon rose, and so did thousands of lightning bugs—a sparkling web of lights greeting the moon as blue ghosts crept along the ground, made possible by my no-pesticides policy. In another year, we were coming home along the state road on a Tuesday night, and a tiny fawn appeared in the headlights. Perhaps a week or two old. It stumbled down the road on spindly legs. Suddenly, Mama burst from the pasture, jumped the fence, and dashed into the woods. A loud snort instructed her baby to get out of the road and it did, leaping into the ditch.

We see deer daily—single does, in pairs with their fawns, in family groups of mother, elder sister (last year's baby), and this year's twins. During the fall rut, herds of ten or twelve are seen. Wallace was charged by an eight-point buck last year down at the gate, and this year, a bold buck strutted up the drive toward the garage right into his face! I watch for the ruffed grouse. In the spring, I see the mother followed by her little chicks and listen for the male drumming on a log in the fall, calling up the ladies to covey. They are careful and shy and it is a treat to see them.

We await the return of life each spring. The first flowers seen are the dandelions, early nourishment for emerging bees and other pollinators, then bloodroot, and daffodils. I have set bags of hybrid daffodils in the perennial beds, but the ones I love the most are a double variety, planted long ago by a woman who must have longed for a sign that winter was passing. Several fallen-down cabins and old homeplaces up and down our creek display this variety. I imagine the woman visiting each dwelling, joyfully sharing her daffodils.

They bloom in the woods and down in our pasture where the old house and barn once stood.

Every day is interesting, from removing a hissing hognose snake out of the garage to watching a huge fifty-pound snapping turtle dig a hole and lay her eggs next to the driveway. Life is good and always joyful. We are blessed and thankful to live at Mill Pond Farm.

DEVIANT BEHAVIORS

We have a cat, Mr. Silky, who was born in the back of my closet in Lake Junaluska, North Carolina, eighteen years ago. We love this cat. Rather, I love the cat and my husband Wallace likes, or perhaps only tolerates, the cat. The cat exhibits some behaviors that make it impossible for him to spend the night upstairs with us humans.

Wallace attended a state realtors' conference the other day, leaving on a Tuesday morning and returning the next day at noon. I don't sleep well without my husband beside me. With this in mind, he suggested that I lock the automatic gate, check all the doors in the house, and pull down the shades. He also recommended that Mr. Silky sleep with me for solace. That is where the trouble started. Cats are diurnal sleepers, rising like haints to roam about the premises during the night. Full of a seafood pate entrée, the cat slept soundly beside me until the early morning hours. Unable to sleep, I had been wide-eyed until 4:00

a.m., when I gave myself a stern talking-to and finally dropped off.

The assault began at 5:28 a.m. Silky jumped off the bed, jumped back on, padded heavy-footed up to my face, patted it gently, purred in my ear, licked my cheek, and marched around to the top of the pillow where he stepped on my hair, pulling it out. He then raced down to the foot of the bed while I sworped at him and leaped off with a triumphant "Yow!" This was repeated at fifteen-minute intervals, the time required for me to drop back into an uneasy slumber. The visitations increased in velocity and weight until at the number seven march, claws were out, I was being slapped in the face and bounced upon, and hanks of hair were jerked out.

That was enough! Sleeping was over. I rolled out of bed, accompanied by the waving tail, went into the great room where his dish sat upon the placemat, full of the chicken and tuna entrée I had put in his dish at 10:00 p.m. for middle-of-the night feeding. It was obviously unacceptable. In his earlier years, Silky had wolfed down whole cans of shredded, fileted, and chunked liver, chicken, turkey and giblets, veal, and porky cuts. In the past three years his formerly deadly two pairs of canines had reduced to one-and-a-half teeth. I don't know where they went, they just were no longer there one day. Thus, the processed pate products.

I know we are increasing Ingle's Markets and Chewy's profit margins. There are upstairs shelves and basement shelves stocked with hundreds of cans rejected by the cat. Perhaps one day he will come to favor food other than shrimp and whitefish. So we keep it, all of it. Every four to five days I purchase a half pound of low-sodium turkey at the deli. He refuses dry kibble but will eat the three-ounce packages of expensive cat treats; some species of yogurt I think. He sits at our sides at every meal, begging for a hand-out. He doesn't always like people seasoning such as curry and red pepper, but he wants to try it anyway. We have come to call him "Head of Household," and sometimes "Chief Manipulator."

But back to the sleepless night steadily advancing toward dawn.

I picked up the bowl of chicken and tuna, scraped it into the trash can, closed up his portal to the basement, and opened the stairwell door. I called him. I won't tell you WHAT I called him. He ran back into the bedroom to hide. I pursued and helped him out from under the bed, putting him on my shoulder. He began to purr, which almost defeated me right there. Resolutely, I carried him to the door, opened it, and sort of nudged him down the stairs to the fifty-degree basement with no food and no water. He gave me a baleful look over his shoulder. I closed the door and returned to bed.

Here I pause, having confessed to feline neglect. Did I finally sleep? No. I laid there and worried about the cat being cold, hungry, thirsty. At 8:30 a.m. I got up to prepare his breakfast and let him out. He was lying on the top step right next to the door. Probably for warmth, my conscience told me. He sauntered in, waving his tail as though there had been no breach in our relationship and wrapped himself around my legs.

Did I know better than to keep him upstairs all night? Of course.

Were there deviant behaviors displayed on both sides?

I'll leave that up to you.

BEYOND DC

This is a somewhat true story that happened in November of 2013.

I had left Washington, DC, about 7:00 a.m., driven north through Baltimore and into the hills of Northern Virginia. My husband, a realtor, was at an all-day legislative conference in Washington. He and his associates would be on The Hill all afternoon. I was free to roam until I met them at Oceana for dinner.

I can't tell you exactly where I was, only that I passed through wide swaths of forest and green hills before clusters of gray stone and black steel buildings began to appear on both sides of the road. I would call them installations—extensive and massive. Some were surrounded by heavy eight-foot metal fences topped with coils of razor wire and intermittent cameras, and some were fronted by simple four-foot-high stone walls and gatehouses, for most had manned gates. Signs identifying them were set into wide expanses of manicured lawns, and I glimpsed others through thick woods. They all spoke of America's military-industrial might—fortresses, Department of Defense behemoths, huge industries with fat defense contracts. As I drove, I saw frequent signs that stated "US Government Property—Keep Out," and "Authorized Personnel Only." They went on for miles and miles.

Suddenly, and you know how this is, I had an urgent need to find a bathroom. There was no convenience store, no rest area in sight. I needed to find somewhere—fast.

I turned right at the next road. The narrow, winding, concrete drive through thick woods led to a huge black and gray stone building that appeared to stretch through the woods for at least a quarter of a mile. A sign identified it as "Clary Metals Corporation: World Headquarters." It sounded corporate—public and friendly enough. It should be all right to use Clary's bathroom. The uniformed man came out from his little stone hut to record my registration tag. *That's strange, why would someone need my tag number?* I thought.

He waved me through and called, "The bookstore is on the left inside."

Sure, I looked like a student with my earnest, bathroom-seeking expression, faded blue-gray Georgetown sweatshirt, and driving an old, battered Corolla. I checked my rearview mirror and saw him slip a cellphone from his pocket. Clary Metals? Defense contracts probably; maybe it was a sensitive site. Golly, I just needed a bathroom. Then I'd get out of there and continue to enjoy my ride.

I parked at the windowless front and entered through a heavy glass door. It was flanked by two men sterner looking than the gate keeper. I was directed to a glass cube in the center of the lobby. A woman seated inside beckoned to me and asked for my identification. I slid my North Carolina driver's license into the tray. She looked at the photo, then to me, back and forth. She informed me that my ID and my purse would be returned to me when I left. One of the escorts advanced and took my keys and bag without a word. This was also very strange, but I had bathroom—and quickly, now—on my mind, so I didn't give it another thought. The woman admitted me through a steel door to the left with a sharp buzz.

I was in a very large room, a library of sorts, lined with floor-to-ceiling bookshelves. They displayed hundreds, no, thousands of books, DVDs, pamphlets, journals, and scholarly monographs bound in brown file folders. Several shelves bore signs that read, "For Sale." Two doors in this expanse of literature announced "Bathroom" and "Staff Only." At last! I gratefully used the facilities and returned to the library where I browsed for over an hour. Finally, I selected two volumes: *The Proliferation of the Iranian Military and Its Proxies in the Middle East,* and *The Distribution of Congolese Rare Earth Metals.* I was not really informed on these two topics, but I thought they could give me a leg up when playing Trivial Pursuit.

I would have liked to sit at one of the reading tables and get lost for hours, but I was expected to meet my husband at 8:00. I looked around for a staff person—no one. No cash register, no intercom, just a lazy camera eye high up on the wall silently following me around the room. Feeling uneasy, I turned toward the steel door. No handle, no knob. I was starting to condemn myself for not paying attention.

I banged on the door. "Hello? Hello? Ma'am, I need to pay you. I'm ready to leave! I'm ready to go now."

Nothing. I raised my fist to bang on the door again, and with a click and a swoosh, the two escorts? Guards?—I don't know what they were—shouldered in. I backed up, and my books fell to the floor.

"Dr. Serota, please come with us."

What? How do they know my name? Of course, my license, but my credentials were not on it or on anything in my bag. "Come where? Why?"

"This shouldn't take long."

My mind busily processing, I noticed both men were at least six feet two inches, wearing identical dark suits and buzz cuts. *Who are they? Maybe I should not have turned down this drive.* My scalp began to prickle.

"Are you FBI? What do you want with me?"

"This way, please."

Another click, and I was ushered through the "Staff Only" door into a long, dimly lit hallway. It was lined with card slots and fingerprint readers mounted on identical steel doors. Cameras were installed at intervals high up on the walls, and their red lights clicked on as we passed. The three of us were buzzed into a large, bare room with a table and three chairs. I began to have thoughts of Central American dictators' interrogation rooms and swallowed hard. The single chair was pulled out for me and I sat down, assisted by a rough hand on my shoulder. The two men, now officially "guards" in my mind, stood right behind me. I heard them breathing over my head. I didn't like this at all, but sensed I needed to keep my wits about me and not show fear. The Bible verse from 2 Timothy ran through my mind and I clung to it: "For I have not the spirit of fear, but of love and power and a strong mind." I was not feeling like embracing love in this situation, but I focused on the power and the strong mind and breathed deeply.

Two more men, physical brothers of the guards, entered the room and sat in the chairs facing me across the table. One smiled thinly; the other's gimlet eyes locked onto mine.

"Just a few questions—Edieth Anne Catherine Yael Serota Scott Shealy—so many names. What is your real name?"

"Well, all of them at different times for different purposes," I replied.

"Different purposes? Your license says you are Catherine S. Scott, living in North Carolina, but your work badge identifies you as Catherine S. Shealy working in Tennessee three hours from your North Carolina address. These are interesting discrepancies."

I was startled and did not know where to start. Before I could explain—

"Your file says you were born Edieth Catherine Serota."

My file? It's obvious they had gone through my bag, but—my file? Ah, yes. My memory ticked back to my only arrest, in August, 1968, Lincoln Park in Chicago. I was thrown into the slammer with dozens of other college students because we were protesting for Eugene McCarthy's candidacy outside the Democratic National Convention. I remembered the police telling us we would be documented by the FBI and thinking the police were just trying to scare us. Perhaps it had been true after all, but that was fifty years ago! I was not feeling good about this.

"Would you tell me why I'm here? What do you want?"

"We are interested in why you came here, your names, and in your selection of reading materials."

"Ohhh, I needed a bathroom, that's all. Then I started looking through your library. I read widely on a variety of topics, and . . ." My voice just trailed off.

Their expressions were solemn, and they didn't blink. Let me tell you—that dried me right up. I looked from one to the other and sensed the two behind me had moved closer. I looked toward the door—no handle, no knob. I visualized hypodermics, sodium pentothal, and perhaps torture.

"Your mother was a research associate at the National Science Foundation. What exactly did she study?"

"The sex life, the genetics of trilliums. It's a plant that grows here, in the Appalachians. Why?"

"We don't think so."

"Well, you're wrong. I was in the field collecting plants with her for years, all up and down these mountains, and I was in her lab at the university." Uneasiness was turning to confusion, and fear was creeping in around the edges of my "strong mind." What did they think they knew, and why?

"Your father spoke five languages, yes?"

"My Dad? His parents were Polish and Hungarian and he grew up in a German and Eastern European immigrant community in Texas." I was incredulous they had information about my parents. Did they have files on them too? Was it true what people said, that my government was spying on her citizens?

"Now you are telling the truth, but why didn't you mention he spoke Yiddish and that he was involved in a displaced persons camp after World War Two?"

What on earth was this all about? The only thing that possibly resonated in my mind was the fact that my family is Jewish. I did not like the direction this was heading.

"And you have applied for an Israeli visa to join the Israeli Defense Forces, according to the State Department."

I was getting mad. The fear was gone and I was spluttering. "Yes, I am going to Israel in the spring, but the IDF Reserves only go to fifty-five and I'm aged out. I'm going as a volunteer; the program is called Sar El. You should check that out instead of making lame accusations. And Israel is our ally in the Middle East. What do you possibly find wrong with a citizen visiting Israel?" I was furious and shaking and cold. Was this antisemitism or ignorance?

Gimlet Eyes' stare continued to drill into me. He narrowed them and spat out, "You are going to join the military of a foreign country. Where are your loyalties, Doctor? I think I know where they are. And what happens if war breaks out? Do you expect the United States Embassy to rescue you?" This last remark contained all the hatred and ridicule he could muster.

I stared angrily right back. "Why, I snap the safety off my weapon. What would you do?" A thoughtless rejoinder that I should not have made.

The other interviewer spoke into a tiny mic affixed to his lapel as Gimlet Eyes continued to stare at me with a lip curled in derision. I heard something about "MPs." And then to me, "You are in federal custody. I am arresting you for spying on the United States. You will be held as a foreign sympathizer!"

I was jerked to my feet by the men behind me and thrust into the muscular grasp of two military police who had charged into the room. They locked handcuffs onto my wrists.

"No! No! I am not a spy!" I burst into furious tears. Then I heard Wallace's voice from a great distance filtering down through the layers of frustration and confusion and fear and anger—great anger. Oh, thank God, he found me. I began to kick and thrash in the iron grip of the two MPs.

"Stop it! Let me go—now! My husband is here. He will tell you I am not a spy. Please, let me go with him."

And then I heard with perfect clarity that dear voice at my ear:

"Good morning, my love. You have kicked me black and blue. That must have been some dream."

THE LITTLE BOBBY CHRONICLES

Bob Scott was introduced to me in September, 1980, when I moved to Haywood County, North Carolina, further west in the Blue Ridge, and we married in April, 1982. He was a true mountain man, knowledgeable about all things Appalachian and capable of building a beautiful log house from scratch like his father and grandfather built using traditional tools. Bob was an early propagator of the rhododendron species, and his backwoods acumen connected seamlessly with my interests and experience in the natural world. We grew Fraser fir Christmas trees, other spruce species, hemlock, and native nursery stock in containers and in the field for many years. He told me stories of his early development in the 1930s when he was called "Little Bobby."

I have taken the flavor of these stories and crafted an authentic picture of the traditional life of Appalachian people during this time. Bob died in January, 2013; however, his stories live on.

LITTLE BOBBY AND GRANDADDY

Little Bobby was born at the confluence of Big and Little Sandy Mush Creeks in Buncombe County. His parents had already brought forth five children, but this pregnancy, Maude Jane's last, was proving difficult. So the family was temporarily living with her parents through her confinement. Maude Jane was born on the creeks and met her husband, Irving, while they were attending Mars Hill College. Her father was a doctor and rode his horse on rounds in Madison County. He handled the baby's birth just fine. When Little Bobby was three years old, the family moved back to Haywood County, building a log house on the top of Beaverdam Gap. Here was a fluke of geography: Beaverdam Gap in Haywood shared a common county line with Madison. Coming together at this top of the world was also Newfound Gap next door to Beaverdam, the apex of Haywood County and Buncombe County.

Three counties tied together at the top of the world. As Little Bobby grew up, this area indeed became the top of his world—his whole world, that is. He could walk from his house on Beaverdam Gap east to Newfound Gap, the head of Hominy Community in about ten minutes. Hominy Creek flowed from springheads on Newfound Gap as Beaverdam Creek flowed from springheads on Beaverdam Gap. He called the pure sparkling waters at the top of Newfound "Blue Creek," and it was his happy place. On the other side, west of Beaverdam Mountain, was Bear Wallow Mountain. He had hidey holes there and if he wished to be hidden and not found, only the hunting hounds could root him out. Bear Wallow was his safe place.

Little Bobby began to explore these places around three years of age. They were totally wild then. The rough roads crossing the two gaps were shaped from the earliest settlers' arrival and they were underscored by the original Cherokee trails. It was the time of the last great livestock drives down to South Carolina. Turkeys, goats, sheep, cattle, and hogs were driven from Hot Springs in Madison County and points west in Tennessee and Kentucky down into Clyde, where pens and boarding houses along the Pigeon River provided a night's respite from the hard drive. At one point around the turn of the century, some twenty years before Little Bobby's birth, a drover had fallen out with one of his companions while crossing Beaverdam Gap, dishonoring the man's sister or some familiar human kerfuffle, and his fellow drovers had hanged him on Bearwallow. Little Bobby would hike there and gaze in wonder at the huge white oak hanging tree, still standing. Around the time of Little Bobby's birth, the fast-spreading chestnut virus had arrived in the Southern Appalachians, devastating the huge broad canopy trees that constituted a third of the Appalachians' woodlands. One by one, the giants were infected and fell to the earth. A grown man could stand beside one of them and the trunk would stretch way above his head. By the time Little Bobby began his wanderings, most of these had been dragged out to local sawmills by teams of oxen and mules. A few remained, however, and the rotting logs became home to mammals and reptiles.

I like to say that our mountains are piles of rocks held together by a small amount of very rich humous-y soil. Kind of like a fruitcake. Excavate the rocks for a field and over the winter they appear to propagate a new crop of rocks in the spring. The action of repeated freeze-and-thaw brings this about, and anyone who has tried to farm the heights knows this very well. The successful farmers had bought up the lowlands, where the dirt was the product of topsoil deposited through flooding and added to over the centuries.

The tops of both Beaverdam and Newfound Gaps were largely outcroppings of strangely shaped, huge stones standing like sentinels and left naked through centuries of erosion. In fact, the ingress to Newfound from Beaverdam was through a narrow passage of tall, immoveable stones that met at the top, creating a species of tunnel. Little Bobby passed through there almost daily on his way to the head of Blue Creek. He did not notice anything remarkable about the passage until one cool October morning. He was going along, just entering the rock tunnel, humming an old ballad his Granny MacIntosh had learned him. He heard a rustle like a breeze stirring up dry leaves—only there were no leaves on the rocks above him and no breeze.

He stopped and looked up. He saw a huge timber rattler, the grandaddy of all timbers, poised on the rock top, drawn back to strike, giving a momentary warning with his rattle. Grandaddy had been soaking up warmth from the stone in the sunshine and did not take kindly to Little Bobby's presence. Bobby quickly calculated Grandaddy was around five feet long and as thick in the middle as his father's forearm. His big boffy head swayed back and forth trying to get a good bead on Bobby.

What to do?

If he stood still the snake would surely strike him. If he chose to move, the snake would surely strike him. He chose to hurl himself to the ground where the snake could not reach and began to inch backwards on his belly through the rock tunnel toward the safety of Beaverdam. The rattling became more furious as if the snake was fussing; he had missed a good hit. Little Bobby knew rattlers did not use their venom unnecessarily—they saved it for prey—and wondered why the snake had chosen to threaten him. When he was out of range, he got to his feet and shakily ran back to his house. He knew he had escaped certain death and wanted the comfort of his mother and father. Besides, he could not wait to describe Grandaddy. He might even make him a little longer and a bit stouter.

His mother, oldest siblings, and his father's brother were out in the yard when he got back. They were hauling the big iron boiling pot from the shed to a heavy iron grate placed over a fire just made. A small mountain of sweet cane stalks lay by the hand-cranked crushing machine. It was molasses-making day. Little Bobby's mouth began to salivate, imagining the thick sweet syrup dripping from his mama's hot buttered biscuits. His mind dwelt on all the delightful images of molasses-making and he temporarily forgot about Grandaddy.

"Come over here, Bobby," said his mother. "You're big enough to help this year. You can feed the crusher."

This suited him just fine. He was eager to help and envisioned himself heroically pushing the stalks through the machine, seeing them split and the sweet juice coursing into the pot. Perhaps he could help stir with the big ash paddle, too. It was important to keep the thickening juice moving around the pot. There was nothing worse than boiled, burnt syrup. Seeing the syrup moving in figure eights under the paddle in his mind's eye brought back the sway of the snake's head. His mind felt gingerly around the memory. He was no longer afraid of the timber rattler. He began to appreciate the beauty of the rust-colored stripe that ran down the middle of Grandaddy's back, the narrowing black velvet tail, the tip of ivory rattles, and even the big venom-filled boffy head. Grandaddy was a beauty and a survivor. A magnificent hunter and focused killer. He belonged right where he was. On the rocks, the king of his country.

Bobby decided he would not tell his father about the snake. His father would take a long-handled hoe to the tunnel and kill Grandaddy. Bobby began to see himself as Grandaddy's guard, his safety. That was far better than his executioner. Perhaps he would see the snake again. He would be more careful when he passed through the tunnel.

This was the beginning of Little Bobby's awareness of and love for all living things. He understood early on that everything on his mountain paradise somehow magically belonged together, worked together, and that he was their protector. As Bobby grew older, this understanding would undergird his life and give meaning to all his decisions. He would become a writer and a champion of the natural environment.

And it all began with a confrontation with an ancient timber rattler he called "Grandaddy."

LITTLE BOBBY AND THE SCHOOL BUS

The early September morning was already heating up. Steam was rising in the harvested cornfields of Beaverdam Valley. It was the first day of school, the day after Labor Day, 1936, and Little Bobby was nowhere to be found. He had sneaked out of the family's log house atop Beaverdam Gap at dawn. He had the run of the mountain and was a wild little thing, preferring the woods of the Beaverdam and Hominy communities to staying around the home place. He had a natural affinity for all growing and living things—animal, vegetable, and mineral—and the spirit of an explorer. He sometimes rode John, his father's huge, long-eared, gray plowing mule, or he "legged it" on his travels.

"Well, there goes Little Bobby. I wonder if Maude Jane knows he's busted out again," commented the neighbor women. They watched the six-year-old boy canter by, his legs sticking straight out, a mere speck on the broad back of John the Mule. Bobby had never been off the mountain or to town where the paper mill smoked day and night. The mountain was his domain, and he did not wish to leave it.

But John the Mule was in the barn. Brother Jack was sent running to check Little Bobby's hidey holes over on Bear Wallow Mountain. He found him and pulled Little Bobby out, hollering and fighting, and quick-marched him home for a fast wash and change into clean overalls.

His mother thrust a poke at him containing fried side meat in two cold cathead biscuits left over from breakfast and an apple for his lunch. "Now you, Bobby, you behave yourself and do what the teacher tells you, just like we talked about. And you, Jack, I'm holdin' you to account to get 'im there."

Jack took a firm grip on Bobby's shoulder and the two of them raced down the mountain to meet the bus at Edwards' Store, the community's gathering place.

The bus was the main reason Little Bobby had taken off to Bear Wallow. His brothers and sisters had described the conveyance in horrifying analogies of fire-breathing dragons, smoking furnaces, and a big-mouthed hungry monster with an appetite for tender little boys. Little Bobby had already concluded he would not live long enough to reach school, so he had determined the monster would not catch him.

He and Jack fetched up to a knot of boys and girls standing in front of Edwards' Store. Little Bobby was resourceful and he had a plan. He looked up at Jack with his most fetching and winsome expression. "Has ye got a penny?" he asked Jack.

"Oh no you don't." Jack knew Bobby would disappear into the cool dim interior of the store and scoot through the back door into the chicken yard. Scattering piglets, goats, and hens ahead of him, he would scale the fence, unseen, and thus run on to the Bear Wallow. He would not be so easily found this time. Jack and Little Bobby would get a switching and maybe worse. Jack held tightly onto Bobby's shoulder.

And then, there it was—chugging and clanking out of a dark, gray, greasy cloud of smoke. OH NO!! Little Bobby's mouth fell open and he clapped his hands over his ears. He had never seen or heard or smelled anything like it. It was dark metal, black, huge, ugly, and belching oily smoke like a creosote-encrusted chimney. There was a horrible grinding noise like the tub mill on the creek that ground his family's corn and wheat between two giant stones—only this was louder and more violent! The black monster shook all over like it was going to jump at him. It came to a shuddering stop with an ear-splitting fart from a pipe sticking out of its rear end. Now he knew it was alive!

Little Bobby saw children's faces at the windows; they seemed to be screaming for help. His eyes popped out and he started backing up. The lips of the door popped in the middle and they flew open with a loud *CLANG!* The mouth of the beast opened wide—for him. He wheeled around to run and Brother Jack caught him by the arm.

"Now, Little Bobby, don't do that. You don't want to be ignorant. We're going to school now—come on and act right!"

"No! No! NO! I AIN'T A-GONNA DO IT!" Little Bobby twisted and jumped to get free. Jack grabbed him by the galluses, biting and kicking. "Let me loose! I'll not be eaten by that thing!"

Two older boys stepped forward to seize him.

Mr. Crocker, the driver, hollered, "Let him go, boys—there'll be more trouble for all of you'uns absent for chasin' him than for one sniffly-nosed little kid! I'll send the truant after him."

Little Bobby gave the man sitting in the monster's front a terrified look, dropped his poke into the dirt road, turned tail, and beat it back up Beaverdam Mountain as fast as his little legs would carry him. He didn't look once behind to see if anyone was chasing him and did not stop until he reached Bear Wallow. He squirreled up a tall chestnut oak and straddled a limb twenty feet up. Panting and shaking, he pressed his little tear- and sweat-stained cheek against the cool bark of the tree trunk. He did not know who or what a "truant" was, but he kept watch and hid out the rest of the morning.

Hunger alone drove him out of the tree and home around one. Mama Maude Jane found him in her kitchen. He was hooking cold biscuits from the warming shelf on the back of the wood cook stove.

Little Bobby began to sob. "It was Mr. Crocker in the belly of that thing, Mama. I'd reckoned he was a nice man. But I won't go to school—I won't! I won't, I'll be ignorant. But I won't go—I'll run away." He panted and looked up at his mama, tears making dirty little rivulets down his cheeks.

Maude Jane set her hands on her hips and looked down at her little son. She regarded him with a mixture of anger, frustration, bewilderment, and pity. He was so dirty and looked so starved and wild-eyed she could not bring herself to punish him. She poured a glass of cool buttermilk and added apple butter to the biscuits. "Don't you leave the yard now," she cautioned.

He moped around the rest of the afternoon, half-heartedly making plans for a life elsewhere, waiting and dreading for Jack and his Daddy to get home and romp on him.

That evening his father rode his horse in from preaching a service over in Madison County. Maude Jane described Little Bobby's behavior. He shook his head and swallowed his laughter as he sought out the runaway.

"You gonna strop me, Daddy?" His eyes were filling up with tears, for Little Bobby loved his father more than anyone else.

"No, Son, we're going to have a talk about school and that bus."

The following morning, Little Bobby obediently trotted down the mountain with his siblings, quaking inside, but putting on a brave and manly show as he had promised his daddy. He joined the other children in front of the store and apprehensively looked down the road toward town. The beast appeared out of its cloud of smoke and fumes. Little Bobby squeezed his eyes shut and swallowed hard. He climbed the steep steps through the mouth of the monster, nodded to Mr. Crocker, walked down the long aisle, and took a seat at the back window. The beast began to lurch around in the road and slowly chug forward.

He turned around and watched the clarity of his magical and carefree babyhood on the mountain disappear in a cloud of black, oily smoke.

LITTLE BOBBY AND THE GIRL IN THE ATTIC WINDOW

Little Bobby was born into the rarified atmosphere of the Sisterhood. This was the three high peaks of northern Haywood County: Newfound, Beaverdam, and Bear Wallow. They were mostly wild then, and so was he, roaming the mountains unrestrained and free. Free, that is, until age six when he met the diesel-fuming monster that ferried him to public school at Beaverdam Elementary. This daily excursion broadened his horizons to the deep-soiled Beaverdam Valley, the kingdom of prosperous farming families, unlike the root hog or die people of the heights he came from.

The largest home in the valley belonged to the third-generation Schellenberg family. The two-story, gabled, white frame structure crowned a small rise in the middle of the holding, dominating the 300 acres that stretched up the slopes of opposing ends and cut a swath across the valley, east to west. Rich fields were centered in the flats created by the creek that eroded the heights and washed down productive topsoil. Both sileage and sweet corn there grew twelve feet high, and the hay fields were lush with grasses, alfalfa, and red clover that rolled in green waves with the wind.

Adjacent to the house was the huge red Dutch barn giving shelter to six two-horse teams, three teams of long-eared mules, and a dozen rat-control cats. The lofts were swollen with hundreds of hay bales, each weighing forty pounds and hoisted up by means of a pulley affixed to the peak of the roof. Three tall sileage silos reached for the sky next to the barn. A smaller barn nightly held forty sturdy black-and-white Holsteins that provided milk to sell and three Jersey cows with dainty ankles that gave gallons of rich butterfat milk and cream for the family.

The sleds, wagons, and family carriage lived in a shed built onto the side of the cow barn. There was also one experimental blue Ford tractor of early simple structure, regarded suspiciously by the horses and mules. Farmer Schellenberg was always looking for the latest farming development and often called for the local agriculture agent's opinion.

First-generation woodlands dominated the slopes at either end of the holdings and were selectively cut for the sawmill in town. Using good management practices, three trees were planted from the nursery down by the creek for every mature giant cut. Oak, hickory, hard rock maple, ash, and locust logs were harvested and the laps sawed up and sold as firewood.

So it could be said, rightfully, that the Schellenberg family was prospering and led an exemplary life filled with good fortune and contentment. This was not entirely true, however. For hidden away in the third-floor attic was the small, sad wraith of a girl, Rachel, diagnosed with consumption. This was the label of tuberculosis in the 1930s, and there was no cure. The disease attacked the lungs, and the constant coughing brought up a bloody flux. It was also called the wasting disease, for it sapped the body of strength and vigor and ended ultimately in death. Consumption was contagious, the bacillus airborne and transmitted through particulates expelled by coughing. Thus, eight-year-old Rachel was consigned to the attic room. Her meals were brought up on a tray and left outside the door. Each morning, she carried the slop jar and the bloody handkerchiefs in a cloth bag to the door and put them in the hall. They were exchanged for a clean nightgown, hankies, and the jugs of water she used for bathing. The door was her only portal to the outside and a knocking signal was used when these items were exchanged. It had been a year since she was diagnosed, been squirreled away, and had seen a human being in person. She sometimes heard the soft sobs of her mother outside the door and the encouraging, loving statements she made to her only daughter.

There was a gable window in her room, and she sat for hours watching her father, brothers, and the farm hands pass to and fro on their business in the barns. Her view was foreshortened by the side roofs of the house, but in front of her she could see all the way up the valley. Neighbors appeared as small ants scurrying about their chores as the dust rose from Beaverdam Road, winding its way up the mountain to the gap. Rachel had accepted her situation, but she was lonely, so lonely.

Meanwhile, Little Bobby had begun exploring the areas below his home in the gap, bit by bit, all the way down to Edwards' Store, where the school bus stopped. He didn't hike to Blue Creek as often, as there were new worlds to explore. He usually went with his brothers and cousins and bought penny candy from old Mr. Edwards. Sometimes they veered off the road to catch crayfish in the broad, rocky creek and little ringneck and garter snakes they carried home squirming in their pockets to scare their sisters.

They gradually worked their way down to the Schellenberg lands. It was the summer and there was no school. The older boys sought work as farm hands and Mr. Schellenberg hired the older teenagers. He laughed good-naturedly when Little Bobby asked for work.

"You come back when you're fifteen and have some muscles and I'll hire ye."

Little Bobby felt his bicep. It was a bit flabby for sure! "All right," he said. As he turned to walk back home, he caught a movement in the third-story window, a flash of white. How curious, he thought as he trotted home.

A month passed before he remembered that strange movement in the window. He asked his older brother Jack if he had seen it.

"Don't tell me ye saw a haint!" laughed Jack.

"I might've. But I did see somethin'."

"You're off your rocker, Bobby," retorted Jack.

Now we know Little Bobby was full of curiosity, and he was not going to let the matter lie. He was going back to see for himself what that flash of white could be. He just had to know! But first, he needed information. So he started with his mother. He found her at the kitchen table, patting out biscuits for supper while pots steamed fragrantly on the wood cook stove.

"Mama, do you know those people in the big white house down yonder?" He pointed down the valley.

"The Schellenbergs. Yes, I know them. Why? Do you go to school with their boys?"

"No'm. Theys all older'en me. I's just wonderin' is all."

Little Bobby was a guileless child, but for some reason he didn't know, he felt he had to step carefully. His mother was in a conversational mood and Little Bobby was her favorite. He sat down across from her and cradled his chin in his hand, his listening posture. Maude Jane told him that her mother, Bobby's Granny MacIntosh, was one of the last mountain women who knew the ancient secrets of roots and herbs, knowledge shared by the native Cherokee women and passed down. Granny helped women through childbirth and she nursed the sick.

"Eight years ago, Mrs. Schellenberg birthed her last child, a little girl. The only girl child in a family of four boys. How she had longed for a little girl! They called her Rachel for the wife that Isaac loved, in the Bible." She smiled, remembering. "Your Granny was called to birth her, but your Grandpa had taken her in the wagon over to White Oak the day before to help another woman, and they were still there when Mr. Schellenberg came to the house. You were just a little'un, a year old—crawlin'—and don't remember that."

"No." Little Bobby didn't remember. He was eyeing the plump biscuit dough he loved. His mother pinched off a piece for him and continued.

"Mr. Schellenberg asked could I come, as I had been to a few birthings with your Granny. His wife would want another female there, and your daddy said, "Yes, go help her." So, I got up on the horse behind him—law, that was one big creature—and we went—fast! I still remember that ride.

Mr. Schellenberg brought that baby himself. He had pulled many a calf and a colt and he knew what to do. Besides, it was her fifth baby, and it was a quick and easy birth. I stayed to nurse Mrs. Schellenberg until your Granny got back. I think we got to be friends during that week. She was happy to have another woman around with all them five menfolk. And her husband paid me a good handful of foldin' money, too. After that, they called me when someone in the family took sick, and I've been there many a time. I was there when little Rachel first . . ." Her voice trailed off and her face fell into sadness. "Goodness me." She looked at the little watch pinned to her bosom. "I'm late puttin' these biscuits in. Go on now, it's almost suppertime. Go call your daddy and your brothers and sisters."

Bobby went out on the porch and sat down on the front steps, pondering everything his mother had said. He was happy the two families had some connection, but he was puzzled by his mother's sadness. He also knew he had never seen a sister at school with her brothers. A sister who would be in the grade below him. Where was she? More curiosity and more unanswered questions. He didn't think to call anyone for supper.

He was deep in thought when his mother came out. "Little Bobby! Do I need to get a switch?"

He sought out his older brother the following week. Jack was friends with the younger two Schellenberg boys. He would have more information, and if Little Bobby was careful, he could get it out of him without being teased to death. That was the usual way Jack did business with his younger brother. Little Bobby had thought and thought about someone else he could ask. Not a grownup; he felt he had exhausted the information his mother would offer. He could hear her saying, "That's none of your business—let it lay." His father probably would not know anything. That left Jack, the thirteen-year-old brother he felt closest to, despite the teasing.

He caught Jack out in the front yard, sitting in the tree swing, with a dreamy look on his face. *He's thinkin' of some ole girl.*

Little Bobby took a deep breath and suddenly appeared in front of his brother. "Jack, you recollect when we went down to the Schellenbergs an' you got your job? Do you 'member askin' me if I had saw a ghost? It t'weren't no haint. It was someone in the attic winder watchin' us."

Jack looked at Little Bobby open-mouthed. "Why, that was Rachel, their little sister. She's sick and stays up there so no one'll catch it."

"Catch what?"

"Some breathin' ailment."

Little Bobby cogitated on this for a moment, wondering what it must be like to be stuck up in that attic all alone. It must be just awful. The same compassion he had for Grandaddy Timber Rattler and for the barn cats and groundhogs and possums and his pet raccoon began to stir within him. He began to think how he could connect with her, bring her some cheer. He wanted to be her friend. But how? This would take even more thought, and his brow furrowed. He looked up to see Jack watching him, close-like. He quickly decided he would risk coming clean.

Little Bobby took another deep breath. "Jack, it must be hateful to be stuck up thar all by yerself. She cain't have any friends. I wanna do somethin' to help her. I wanna be her friend, but I don't know how." He looked appealingly at Jack with the expression he knew would touch his brother's heart. At least he hoped it would.

And it did. Jack also began to think. He had not realized what life must be like for Rachel since she was hidden away and her brothers didn't talk about her. It was almost like she was dead and buried.

"Ya know, I could git my berry-pickin' basket an' pass it up to her with notes an' leetle gifts like . . . like purty rocks an' pinecones an' moss. Maybe you'd gimme some of yore comics when yer done with'em. I figure she's eight years old an' she could read a mite afore she got sick. Maybe she could send me a note back," Little Bobby was getting excited now. The possibilities were growing fast.

"How could you pass it up to her? She'd need a rope or somethin' like to haul it up an' down. Lemme think about it, Bobby. Don't bother me none. Go on now."

Little Bobby went on in the house, climbed the ladder into the boys' loft bedroom, and looked out the window to the big white house far down the valley. The attic window, Rachel's window, was tiny, but he imagined her standing there, looking up at his window. Jack would help him, and he would help her.

Monday was a workday at the Schellenberg farm, and Little Bobby's brothers left after breakfast to walk down the mountain. Jack had asked Little Bobby to bring his basket and come with them. He trotted along, wondering what Jack had in mind. He had passed the weekend mindful not to bother Jack while he was thinking.

When they arrived at the barn, Mr. Schellenberg gave out work assignments for the morning and saw Little Bobby standing behind the boys. "I thought I told ye to come back when ye growed some more," he laughed.

Jack said he had just walked down with them and would be going back shortly. Walking was good for his little brother—he'd get strong faster—and he might walk down with them on some other mornings.

"That's fine, just don't get in the way. The horses are big and dangerous, and you might get hurt."

Mr. Schellenberg turned and went into the barn. Jack pulled Little Bobby aside and told him to go stand under the window, but out in the yard a piece. When Rachel looked out, Bobby was to lift the basket up toward her, point to it, lift it up again, and repeat this several times. She would have to figure out how to drop a rope or something to tie to the basket handle. Bobby stood in place and a few minutes later, she did appear in the window. She saw him standing there and watched his strange maneuvers curiously. Then she understood and nodded her head. She waved and Bobby waved back. He then turned and walked out of the yard to the road and started for home. Rachel stood and watched him getting smaller and smaller until he reached Edwards' Store, then he turned left up the mountain and disappeared. That night she went to bed smiling to herself, wondering what would happen next.

Two days later, Bobby again walked down the mountain with his basket. This time, it held a short note: "My name is Bobby and I wanna be yore frend here is a leetle gift fer ye." A small white quartz crystal lay inside on a bed of green moss. He stood in his place until she looked out. The window opened about six inches and a stout piece of red yarn tied to a cardboard cone for weight fell out and tumbled down. Bobby quickly tied the basket to the yarn, tucked the end with the cone inside the basket, and Rachel yanked it up. The empty basket came back down, he untied it, and she again pulled the yarn and cone up. She waved, wearing a big smile, and closed the window. He waved back and started for home. This time, he looked back every few steps to wave at the slight form in the window until he could not see her any longer.

This small act of kindness and friendship continued for three weeks until Mrs. Schellenberg looked out to see a strange little basket tied to red yarn ascending past her second-story bedroom window. She looked down, saw Little Bobby rooted in place, then dashed up the stairs to the attic door.

"Rachel, Rachel! What are you doing?"

"Mama, it's Bobby. He is sending me notes an' gifts in the basket. An' I send him notes back."

She was entirely guileless and open about what they were doing. She told her Mother that they were friends and he was the only friend she had. Please, please, could she keep him? Mrs. Schellenberg thought about her daughter's sparse life in the attic room and about her illness. She instructed Rachel to wash her hands good before she handled the yarn and to be careful not to sneeze or cough on the yarn and the basket. She was glad Rachel now had a friend. She heard her daughter behind the door laugh for the first time in a long time, a sound of pleasure and gratitude and hope.

Mrs. Schellenberg walked outside to the barn where big-eyed Little Bobby still stood and asked him to come with her to find her husband. Little Bobby was trembling, terrified that he was in big trouble, and Jack too. The couple talked right in front of him and they agreed Bobby and Rachel should continue to communicate via the little basket with Mrs. Schellenberg's cautions in place. Mr. Schellenberg asked Bobby to get permission from his parents also to continue.

The Bobby and Rachel friendship continued over her remaining fourteen months of life, with many notes and 'leetle gifts' being hauled up. Rachel constructed a tableau on her dresser of the gifts that no one saw during her lifetime: banks of plush moss, beautiful oddities of rocks and pinecones, interesting sticks covered with red and blue lichens, Little Bobby's drawings of all the things he loved in nature, and a self-portrait of sorts. Jack's worn comic books found a home in the attic room. Rachel expanded her activities with crayons and pen and ink drawings on paper that her mother set outside the door. She was busy drawing and constructing and arranging, when before she had sat empty-handed and listless in her room. Little Bobby gave her a taste of the outside world and the warmth of his companionship until one cold January morning on his way to school, she did not come to the window. He saw the doctor's horse tied up outside the front porch and he knew his special friendship was ending.

Little Bobby and his parents went to her wake at the Schellenberg home, and a little berry basket joined the flowers covering her coffin. She was buried in the Beaverdam Cemetery, and Bobby would drop by to place pretty rocks on her grave. He kept a folder of their shared notes and drawings into his latter age, when everyone called him "Old Bob."

LITTLE BOBBY'S SUMMER VACATION BUSTER

I don't know what a "buster" is to you, but to me it's a grand be-all and end-all event folks remember for a long time.

This is a true story about a man who lived in Haywood County. We all called him Little Bobby" because he was a bit, shall we say, undersized for his age. When we enter the story, he is eleven years old. Although he was small, he was the leader, because he had all the ideas and a big imagination. His busy mind more than made up for his small stature.

One sunny May morning, Little Bobby gazed, chin in hand, through the fifth-grade classroom windows that arched above the steam radiators to the ten-foot ceiling. He focused not on the spelling words written on the chalkboard, but on the inspiring view of the high Balsam Mountains. He was not interested in his schoolwork. His mind was busily devising mischief and daring adventures.

A whole school term's-worth of day-dreamed plans would play out during summer vacation, abetted by his brothers and cousins. His extended family lived on 300 acres atop Beaverdam Mountain. Little Bobby's house sat in the gap, half in Haywood County, half in Buncombe County, with a view north to Leicester and Big and Little Sandy Mush Creeks. To the south lay the prosperous valley farms of the Schellenbergs and the Renos. Five miles beyond smoked the stinking stacks of the Champion Paper Mill. "Smells like money," said the people, and it did. It was the end of the Great Depression, and jobs at Champion had brought the community through.

The next ridge over from Beaverdam was Bear Wallow Mountain, covered in dense woods and massive stone outcroppings. It was the boys' meeting place and hide-out.

Little Bobby put several of his school term daydreams into action over the summer break.

The boys installed Old Man Ferguson's nanny goat into new quarters atop the milking shed.

Uncle Doug had a large dairy farm and a barn with a resident black snake for rodent control. His wife, Eva Jean, did not go out to the barn. She didn't like snakes, so if she needed Doug, she rang the dinner bell hanging on the front porch. Eva Jean cooked on a big woodburning cookstove in the kitchen. She used the water reservoir, a rectangular iron box sauntered on the side of the stove, to boil water for cooking, cleaning, and bathing. One Tuesday afternoon Eva Jean came home from a Ladies Missionary Society meeting to fix supper. She stuffed wood into the stove and fired it up. Hearing a sloshing sound in the reservoir, she stepped over, lifted the lid, and met the black snake reclining in a warm-water bath. The lid went flying; Eva Jean boiled out of the house in a tizzy, screaming her head off. She didn't know which way she was going, but she was going, and she was gone for three days.

Reuben Schellenberg's pair of prize-winning grey horses sported bright blue hooves and orange striped manes and tails. They won no customary blue ribbons at the county fair that summer. They stayed home and hung their heads in shame.

One of the boys' favorite activities was hiding in the roadside haystacks and leaping out and shouting at little girls passing by, sending them home squalling to their mamas.

But I don't want you to think Little Bobby was completely naughty. On the positive side of the slate, he sat with his Granny Maney on her porch and strung and broke green beans on several July mornings without complaint. Granny told him stories about her girlhood on the mountain in the olden days while beans and fatback simmered on the cookstove. He defended the barn cats from the yard dogs and made sure they had fresh water and tasty table scraps. Why, he was even seen cuddling them! He engaged in many other good deeds. He helped his mother and siblings stir the big iron pot of apple butter out in the yard. And was that fire hot!

❧

It was the end of August, just a couple of weeks before school reopened after Labor Day. Little Bobby had been studying up on a real buster: an end-of-summer-vacation mischief. He gathered up his three brothers and four cousins, outlined his plan, and gave out assignments. They sniggered and looked slyly at each other.

"Boys, I swan that's a good one!"

"Let's do it!"

They all ran home, peering around house and barn corners to see if they were being observed. They sneaked into their mother's linen presses and snatched snowy white sheets, then to the barns for empty grain tow sacks. The next stop was the homeplace of Uncle Burder and Aunt Eloise. Burder was working extra hours beyond his seven-to-three shift at the mill, and she was out earning her pin money. Eloise plucked the soft down from the breasts of her barnyard geese and stuffed ticks and pillows. These were prized by the women of the community, and they paid handsomely for them.

The white and grey fowl were Eloise's pride and they also served as sentinels. At the sight of strangers, they would set up a loud honking alarm and run hissing with lowered heads and outstretched necks at the intruders. Uninvited guests lost pieces of their calves and thighs to the geese. Unfortunately for the geese, the boys were judged as known and friendly as they entered the barnyard. The conspirators inspected the birds and advanced slowly.

Working in teams of two, the boys caught eight of them. One boy held the long neck of the goose with one hand and quickly clamped the sharp beak closed with the other. His partner tied the flat, horny feet together and compressed the wings. The geese were one by one thusly disabled and shoved head-first—protesting and honking loudly—into the tow sacks. Once confined, they struggled silently with just an occasional hiss. At the last moment, Little Bobby hooked Uncle Burder's hunting trumpet from its nail in the barn.

Making their way cautiously around barns, houses, and outbuildings, they again avoided exposure. They reassembled on a tall, flat outcropping atop Bear Wallow in the soft darkening of early evening. Below them on the Buncombe County side of the slope were members of a church from Sylva who held a week-long camp meeting on a grassy flat swag each August. The boys laid the sacks on the ground, folded each sheet in quarters, and cut a chunk from the middle with their pocket knives. They then pulled the dazed geese from the sacks, thrust their heads through the holes and freed the wings and legs.

Then, on Little Bobby's count of "one—two—three," they launched.

The church folk were laboring mightily in prayer down below in the swag with the exception of one man sneaking peeks at a comely wider woman. Something caught the corner of his eye and he looked upland to see a heavenly host descending—there—there—and—there!

"Oh, looky thar! Oh looky! Glory oh Glory—it's the angels! They's a-comin!"

The preacher rose from his knees, looked up, raised his arms over his head, and screamed, "Pray saints—pray—for the hour is at hand!"

Some of his flock were staring awestruck with gaping mouths. The descending heavenly messengers were speaking in foreign tongues and the worshippers strained to hear them. Others had flung themselves down into the grass, thrashing around, and shouting. Some, certain the end of days was at hand, were confessing astounding sins heard by human ears for the first time.

Elder Williams shouted, "Forgive me . . . forgive me for lying in lust with Sister Amanda!"

Sister Amanda gasped!

Brother Elmer cried, "I didn't mean to take from the offerin' plate! The Devil was in me that Sunday! Oh! Oh!"

Others chimed in, crying aloud and begging for forgiveness.

Uncle Burder's horn sounded the alarm: *"Ta-ra! Ta-ra!"*

The preacher flung himself headlong into the grass, "Repent! Repent sinners, it's the final Rupture!"

Snatches of thin strangled laughter sifted down from the Bear Wallow pinnacle. The boys were also on the ground, rolling around, nearly breathless with laughter. The preacher looked up and again leaped to his feet as the heavenly messengers landed among the exhorters. They saw not holy angel faces, but the hissing, beak-snapping visages of enraged geese. Tumbling about and dragging the sheets, the vengeful geese stumbled after the worshippers, catching their feet up, tripping, and honking loudly. Scrambling up in disarray, the worshippers fled screaming downhill toward Big Sandy Mush, the furious geese snapping at their heels.

In the midst of this exodus, the preacher extended a long bony finger toward the pinnacle. "You evil boys! You imps from Gehenna! You are consigned to the fiery flames of hell to be bound and tormented for eternity!"

The boys stopped mid-laugh. These imprecations struck on oft-heard Sunday School messages. They jumped up and scattered in divers directions into the woods of Bear Wallow. It took the preacher two hours to round up his bruised and filthy flock, torn and gouged by briars in their rapid descent. Many of them were not speaking to others, but they paid calls on certain mortified Bear Wallow families late into the evening. Fathers and uncles bearing torches snaked up the flanks of Beaverdam, routed boys from their hidey-holes and belts came off.

It took the boys two days to round up all eight geese. The fowl were returned to Aunt Eloise's barnyard after exacting payment for their ordeal from the boys' legs. They did not come along happily with the bitten and bleeding conspirators. Uncle Burder's hunting trumpet was lost for good.

The boys got their proper come-uppance at home too. They spent the last precious week of summer vacation compensating their mothers for the cut-up sheets by sweating over domestic chores meant for girls.

Little Bobby's mischief-making imagination had taken a serious bottom-burning hit. But he was not permanently deterred. He continued to inspire his peers with his adventures, but he never again enacted the Second Coming.

A DIVERSION

We visit Charleston, South Carolina, at least twice every year. The history, architecture, food, and culture are rich and fascinating. Although we are mountain folks from Eastern Tennessee, we love the Lowcountry society that contrasts so vibrantly with our own wonderful world. But the real Charleston pleasure, for me, is part of Plantation Row out on Ashley River Road—the sixty-six-acre John James Audubon Swamp Garden at Magnolia Gardens.

WE ARE SO MUCH LIKE THEM

Back in March, Wallace and I engaged in one of our favorite activities—photographing Lowcountry nesting birds. Outside of Charleston, South Carolina, there is a rare gem on the Ashley River. Magnolia Plantation and Gardens contains a watery sixty-six acre area called the Audubon Swamp Garden.

From Mid-February through mid-April there is a swarm of activity—the courtship, territory-establishing, mating, nesting, and chick-rearing rituals of shore and swamp-dwelling birds. Species include the great blue heron, snowy egret, great egret, little blue heron, wood duck, anhinga, ibis, cormorant and tricolored heron.

There are also many species of songbirds, hawks, owls, gulls, and more that live elsewhere in the swamp; some of them are permanent residents. It's called a rookery and it's like a human village, full of color and chatter and busyness.

The great blue herons are the power magnates and the high-flyers. They stand four-and-a-half feet tall on the horizontal branches of the eighty-foot long leaf pines, solemn sentinels alongside their big messy nesting platforms. They have the best views from their penthouses. The trees grow on small islands in the middle of the lake and on the far side of the swamp. They are all claimed by mid-March. The egrets, anhingas, and cormorants prefer the lower ten-to-thirty-foot levels. There is a condo available for everyone!

The ibis are interesting birds. They look odd with their stout down-turning beaks and they behave curiously. They always maintain their group, whether it's sitting in a tree or foraging together through the marsh grasses. I call them "peer groups." They are shy and humble birds, nesting way back in the swamp. We have never seen their rookery. Several years ago, we documented three ibis; now their flock numbers around twenty permanently residing birds. The Swamp Garden is obviously an ideal location for them.

Anhingas also make their home in the rookery; diving birds who spear fish with their pointed beaks at the end of long expressive necks. They also build rather messy homes and like to sit beside them with glossy black wings outspread in dramatic heraldic poses, drying and warming themselves in the sun. Their calls, harsh "Awk, awks," echo through the swamp. A different species, they live equitably alongside egrets and herons. Like our neighborhoods, everyone together.

We watch a busy pair of great egrets setting up housekeeping on the first floor of a small cypress about twenty feet from shore. Prime photography location for observing a passionate life. They had already selected each other for the season. They are displaying their long, feathery, breeding plumes, which lift like a nimbus of pure whiteness at the slightest breeze. Seasonal partners now, but next year, who knows their preferences? Serial monogamy, like many modern relationships.

They are busy fluffing up the nursery where she will lay three to four eggs and incubate them for twenty-four days, always exactly three-and-a-half weeks. The nest will eventually grow to three feet across, with renovations continuing. Additional sticks, grasses, reeds, and other interior décor items are added. It's kind of like humans, starting small and adding on as the family grows. Himself is bringing home the bacon; flying to the far shore, shopping and bringing home a choice stick for the female's approval. If she doesn't find it worthy, she might fling it into the lake. Sometimes he forages on the ground. Other times, he reaches up to the top shelf of a tree for just the right one.

She watches him approach, rises, and shakes out her beautiful plumage in a lavish display, like a woman dressed in her finest fashions preening for her lover's return. They greet each other on tiptoe, touching chests, entwining their graceful necks, clucking softly.

He presents his offering with a bowed head. She delicately accepts the stick and tries out several arrangements—here—no, over there—yes, exactly right as he watches. They both approve. He then returns to his errands on the shore.

It seems like paradise, but trouble is about to arrive. A lone egret female has been watching from an adjacent tree and flutters over to inspect the construction site. She is looking for a good provider for her progeny-to-be, and this nest looks like an ideal prospective home. Displacement of the resident female is on her mind.

But she is not welcome. In an apparent display of territorial jealousy, Herself rises in a fury from the nest. She attacks the intruder with vicious squawks and powerful stabs of her beak and sharp-toed feet. The intruder is committed to taking the nest and the male, so she also fights furiously. Herself is more committed, having mated longevity in the relationship. Himself watches from the shore as the two females fight it out. He might be injured if he tries to intervene. The neighbors watch with animated interest and join their voices in the melee. Miss Defeated, Rejected, and Lonely is soon seen winging her way across the swamp toward the plantation house. Better luck in another location. The rookery finally quiets down and Himself returns.

Her greeting is effusive and affectionate as she relates the afternoon's gossip. "Did you see that? The nerve of some birds!" She turns her back to him, squats, extends her neck, and offers her tail feathers. They mate again. Their partnership is re-established and strengthened. This repeats over and over again in the rookery, and most relationships endure. But life in the neighborhood is not always lovely.

Enemies lie on the sunning platforms and cruise under the nest trees —hungry alligators waiting to snatch young chicks who wander from home and fall into the water. Red-shouldered hawks fly silently above during the day and the great horned owl attacks nests at night. Raccoons have been known to scale the nest trees and grab chicks. Yellow-bellied sliders are lurking. These smooth-shelled mud turtles also have an appetite for baby birds and can grow to be a foot long!

Life in the nest can be scary. The siblings compete for space, parental attention, and the best morsels. But, like us, they band together against outsiders. Some young birds are lost, but enough survive to continue the life cycles of the species. The Swamp Garden is rich and teeming with life.

It's just as the Creator intended for us and for all living things. We can find many characteristics in which we are so much like them.

HERITAGE

Heritage is constructed of many different aspects of history, cultural mores, stories and music, and the most mundane of everyday activities handed down through generations of families and communities. It can be as simple as the comment, "Well, we've always done it that way," that dries up a child's incessant "Why?" to a shift in environment, religious connections, food preferences, and family structure. New belief strata that are incorporated into time-honored rituals. You may look for evolutions of belief and practice in these very human, very Appalachian, stories.

THE SIN EATER

The practice of eating the sins of the dead was brought over with the earliest Appalachian settlers from Ireland, Scotland, and the Welsh-English border. The practice had been known in the border regions of the British mainland since the Middle Ages.

A sin eater was a person who consumed food placed on the corpse of the deceased. The food eaten was believed to absorb the sins of the deceased, thereby absolving the sin-guilt of the person, preventing their entry into everlasting hellfire and assuring their ingress into heaven.

When a person died, a bell was tolled for every year of their life, calling the community to the home of the deceased. The dead person was laid out on planks placed on a bier, and food and drink was placed on the chest. The sin eater came silently in response to the bell and ate the provisions, thereby appropriating the sins of that person unto himself. He made a pronouncement—"I give easement now to thee and for thy earthly sins dear woman/man, I pawn my own soul"— and slipped away. The mourners in the house turned their backs on him. Taking the sins of the deceased made the sin eater unclean and evil in the eyes of his neighbors. At times, a small amount of money was proffered.

The sin eater was chosen by lots being drawn. The lots contained the name of every male in the community over the age of fourteen. Somehow, he seemed to always end up being a poor person or a recluse whose life was ideally suited to be a hermit. When chosen, he was required to don a dark cloak and a hood with slits for his eyes and a flap for his mouth and live far away from the community. It was considered very dangerous to look upon the face of a sin eater as his soul was contaminated by unspeakable sins of many departed that might be transferred to a living person. His name was never to be spoken. He was known as "The Sin Eater," and any life he had enjoyed prior to his selection was expunged forever. In our mountains, his home was often a cave.

Sin eating became associated with dark magic and superstition, and the sin eaters were outcast from society as voluntary sin eating condemned them to an eternity in hell. The practice of sin eating can be found in ancient Greece and Egypt; it also stems from the Catholic rite of absolution, the forgiveness of sins by a priest as near the time of death as possible. For those who died unexpectedly to be absolved, sin eaters became common in Wales and Ireland in the 1700s and 1800s, with immigrants bringing the practice to the mountains of Appalachia. The mountains were rife with seen and unseen dangers, and it was an easy step to attribute illness, mauling by bears and panthers, known as 'painters', and accidents to the wanderings and influence of evil spirits abroad. In the deepest coves and valleys organized religion did not exist; a memory of God and His judgment persisted from the Old Country, but the sin-atoning work of Christ did not. And so, this taboo practice continued into the 1950s and is said to continue even to this day in the most primitive regions of Southeastern Kentucky, Western North Carolina, Southwestern Virginia and Northeastern Tennessee, along with the practice of snake handling.

Who knows? Perhaps tonight back in the holler, an elderly man or woman has died, or perhaps a little child. The Sin Eater has heard the solemn death bell, has hooded himself and wrapped up in his cloak, and is on his way from his reclusive shelter. Food and drink are being prepared and set out on the cooling slab in the parlor. Mourners are ready to turn their backs and tightly close their eyes. They would not dare to look upon him and chance a transference of sin.

Would you?

MADISON COUNTY, 1969

Between my graduation from Mars Hill College in May and entry into North Carolina State in September 1969, I obtained a grant to complete a housing survey in Madison County, a rural, mountainous, de-populating county in Western North Carolina. I say de-populating because many young men and families relocated to the tank and landing craft factories in Ohio and Michigan during World War II and did not return. The factories reverted to making trucks and cars, and the men stayed. They obtained good-paying jobs for their relatives in the fifties and sixties and more families left.

The aforementioned grant was obtained from the Opportunity Corporation of Buncombe-Madison Counties, the local anti-poverty agency funded by the federal Office of Economic Opportunity. When completed, it would show every habitation in Madison, categorized from "standard" to "dilapidated." There were five classes of housing, and we were required to do a four-page survey with every tenth house. The

Opportunity Corporation would use these statistics in their grant application to the Department of Housing and Urban Development for money to build low-income housing. It was the height of anti-poverty funding in America, and Madison wanted to get its share. The need for standardized housing was so great.

My partner, Paul Scott, and I set off from the southwestern corner of the county in his little Chevy Vega with huge US geological survey maps on my lap. At that time, there were few paved roads, but many, many single-lane rutted dirt roads and lots of goat paths. People lived back in the hollers, so we put on our hiking boots to reach them, often walking two or more miles uphill and back. It was June, July, and early August—hot and dusty. We carried milk jugs of cool water and sack lunches, for cafes were few and far between. The Opportunity Corporation community organization workers had put out the word that we were "okay" and were surveying to help the county get housing.

The area was known as "Bloody Madison" due to internecine warfare and political battles that sometimes escalated to gunfights. The violence had begun during the Civil War, when the county was split between Yankee supporters and Confederate loyalists. One hundred years later, the old animosities continuosly flared up. The Ponder political machine was firmly ensconced in the county seat of Marshall and dispensed patronage in the form of the few county and federally funded jobs. Shelton Laurel and Sodom were two communities known for their pugnacious natures. We were out of there before nightfall.

There were some instances in which either the workers had not okayed Paul and me or the folks just didn't care. We drove up the dirt roads as far as possible and walked up the paths into the woods. The second growth timber was some seventy years old, and the forest was dark under the hardwood canopy. A bold stream always surged from the laurel thickets and rhododendron hells. Sometimes a silent, grim-faced man holding a shotgun stepped out from behind a white oak or poplar and stared menacingly or growled, "That's far enough, young-uns."

That was our cue to turn around wordlessly and skedaddle back down the path. There was moonshine being made up there. We probably missed a few houses, but we didn't get shot. A question mark was noted on the map.

I wrote "1" for a standard house a few times within the town limits of Mars Hill, Marshall, and Hot Springs. Most houses were assessed as a four or five. This was easy because I could see the outhouse perched over the creek. Straight-piping was common practice, and a lot of houses had no electricity either. Paul and I sat in many a cabin or single-wide trailer doing the interview. The trailers were new to the county and sat next to the hundred-year-old pole cabin still used for storage or for an over-flow of visiting children or grandparents. We were invited inside, offered a woven-rush-bottomed straight-backed chair on a puncheon floor, a glass of cool buttermilk from the springhouse, and a dip of snuff.

If the man of the house was present, he silently slipped out and left the survey to the women. We knew he was listening just outside though, and so did the womenfolk, making their answers carefully parsed. These were private people who had no place for "th' gov'ment." Some might call them suspicious—we preferred to call them careful. Many spoke in accents of Middle English, using words found in *The Canterbury Tales*, and they clung to the old ways of living.

"Whet did you ax me? Forthy, don't want that scary old 'lectricit and noon wants the s---house in their abode."

We saw antique tractors from the 1930s in use, and draft horses and oxen used for plowing. Gardens flourished outside the houses, and the occupants sometimes offered us early cucumbers, squash, and lettuce. Cash crops of tobacco, cabbage and potatoes grew on the hillsides, hoed by curious children who gave us the side-eye. We side-stepped chickens, angry roosters, and geese in the swept dirt front yards and suffered their bites. A goose can wring a chunk out of your calf. Hogs and cattle roamed unfenced in the outer areas, feasting on mast in the woods and grass along the dirt roads. They were marked by their owner with notches in their ears. We saw carefully tended flowerbeds in the towns. Out in the country, bright scarlet geraniums and multi-colored zinnias flourished in old coffee cans and lard buckets, brightening the grayness of the dirt yards and sawmill board-lapped houses.

We arrived in Hot Springs, about mid-summer and surveyed down a dirt road that ran along the French Broad River with houses on the upper side. Paul and I parked the Vega and started toward the first house.

A woman sitting on her porch began to holler at us, "Run, run!"

We looked around and saw a six-foot black racer, a constricting snake. It appeared to be chasing us. We ran, but the snake was gaining.

The woman shouted, "Turn aside, turn aside!"

We did, and the snake, intent on its own business, slithered on past us down the road.

This was just one reptile encounter we had. Paul and I approached a run-down farmhouse in the Big Laurel community in late July. Sometimes the houses looked deserted but were not. This one appeared to be a number ten, earning an interview. We stepped up on the porch and Paul fell through three rotted floorboards into the crawl space below. It was definitely a crawl space. Several copperheads were crawling down there, and it was their mating season. With terrified shrieks and expletives, he lifted himself up through the boards, a copperhead clinging to his pants leg. He was fortunately not bitten, and we determined the house was vacant, which made it a three. We learned to carry stout walking sticks. Encounters with the thick-bodied timber rattlesnakes along the goat paths were common, and every creek's deep hole sheltered a snapping turtle.

Madison County in the summer of 1969 largely kept to its old ways, drowsing in the dusty sunlight, tree frogs singing, bees humming. Its citizens resisted new inventions like electricity, telephones, and septic tanks. The southeastern corner of the county was reached; the survey was completed by mid-August. Four tick bites, multiple chiggers, several fights with barnyard geese, two slide-off-the-road wrecks in the Vega, and a flight across a pasture from an angry bull were recorded, in addition to the county's housing structures. The next year, fifteen apartment units in two locations near Marshall began. Fifteen families left the hollers and moved to town.

The new apartments offered electricity, inside water, and a bathroom. The water ran out hot from the faucet! A small sitting-out porch looked out on the road, but the green views of mountain and pasture had been cut off. The walls were painted, not insulated with newsprint and pictures cut out and pasted from magazines. The cook stove did not use wood, and heat was accessed by turning a dial on the wall. No spring-house, but a refrigerator. Suddenly, women's days were simplified and easier. Groceries came from the store downtown, or from the commodities program. Children attended school in a modern brick building with a cafeteria and a playground. Men were idle or sought day labor in town. The apartments were close together, and for the first time, families were an un-welcome witness to the lives of their neighbors. This was not always easily managed. Disapproving looks were exchanged, gossip flourished, and disagreements broke out, even fights. An extra law enforcement of-ficer was hired to manage situations that had not oc-curred on the far-flung farms.

The garden, the barn, the dirt yard, the woodlot, the mountain, and the fields were gone; the old ways were passing. Human beings were now separated from the land and its ways.

Was this progress? Was this a good thing?

I'll let you decide.

THE PANCAKE PRINCESS

I first saw sixteen-year-old Sue Ann standing on the corner of Main Street in a CVS parking lot. She was dressed in a long, acid-green sateen skirt, a bright yellow ruffled rayon blouse and purple rhinestone-embellished high heels. A terrifying cherry-red wig lay on her shoulders, like so many pick-up sticks, and hid her scruffy blond hair. A younger supporter named Darla stood next to her and held up a printed cardboard sign:

Vote for Sue Ann Worley
for Pancake Princess!

Sue Ann wore her Goodwill garb proudly, grinning, and greeting passersby with a slow-drawled, "He-e-ey there!"

In my growing-up southern town, every girl could have her own beauty pageant—the Rhododendron Queen, the Lady of Laurel, the Tomato Princess, the Tobacco Duchess, and the Queen of Corn. There was a pageant somewhere almost every weekend during the late summer and fall in the South.

In Edgewood, Tennessee, they all vie to become the Pancake Princess, a be-all, end-all, take-your-life-in-your-hands scramble that happens to coincide with the YMCA Relay for Life and the all-you-can-eat fluffy carbohydrate breakfast contest. This was no "let's commemorate this flower or that vegetable" jump-up, but a political, carefully organized, stellar community event fueled by fat-wallet papas and frantic mamas yearning to share in the reflected glory of their daughter's success. Hopeful young ladies flocked from Upland and Whitaker to Edgewood to enter the competition, and from every crossroads in between.

Sue Ann had none of this high-powered respecter of persons' backing. She had a scrappy disposition, a courageous little heart, and a creative imagination. She aimed to win.

Her personality had been formed and honed by a root-hog-or-die existence in the backwoods of Rocky Pine Valley, her keen spirit developed early on in desperate competition for a space at the dinner table and enough personal space to breathe. Sue Ann's single-mindedness, interpreted as rebelliousness, earned her hard knocks from the hard-faced and harder-handed males in her large extended family.

But Sue Ann had dreams that stretched far away from Rocky Pine Valley. Her desire for self-actualization was a seductive light at the end of the tunnel, and it summoned her forward. Being crowned Pancake

Princess would be the first entry on her resume. She planned carefully how to proceed. The first step was to get the names of twenty-five supporters on the entry form. That was easy—the town merchants satisfied that requirement with sympathy signatures. The next was sponsorship, which was also no problem. The hardware store that sold the men in her family their extensive gun collection felt obliged. The manager paid the fifty-dollar entry fee. Her older sister Pat, owner of Patty's Pretty Parlor, offered to do her hair and makeup. Her wardrobe? Back to Goodwill. She scoured the racks for a gown to match the purple rhinestone heels. Success! A black-and-purple-striped, plunging neckline, jersey maxi-dress showed off to perfection the curves she DIDN'T have. Next, she dived into the twenty-five-cent, last-chance grab bin and came up with a shimmery orange Lurex swimsuit for the swim competition. She tried it on.

Bless her heart! Her pale beanpole figure looked just like an orangesicle.

But Sue Ann was not discouraged. She knew she had the talent category, and that carried weight. Her singing abilities were hidden to all except her sister Pat and her mother. The voice of a lark with a two-octave range, amazing musicality, and impressive breath control. She practiced nightly in the bathroom as the shower emptied the water reservoir. You may remember the song she chose, "You Light Up My Life." It accented her skills to perfection. Her voice soared up to a bell-like high C and descended with perfect pitch to a melodiously throbbing tenor G. Her vibrato was subtle and accentuated the emotive lyrics perfectly. Never taught, uncoached, she was a musical ingenue yet undiscovered—a mountain songstress from Rocky Pine Valley, Tennessee.

The night arrived, and the Edgewood High School auditorium had standing room only. The folks the fire marshall kept turning away stood out in the schoolyard. The crowd was expectant and noisy. The pageant was about to start.

Sue Ann joined the clutch of prancing, beautifully gowned and coiffed young women backstage. They checked out her blond Shirley Temple ringlets and the purple-and-black dress. There were a few insulting stares and snide remarks exchanged behind gloved hands. Sue Ann was no competition—her dowdy presence served as a sad backdrop that accentuated their superior qualities. Her appearance had been the object of their ridicule since first grade. And besides, everyone knew you wore powdery pastels to these events!

The contestants paraded before the judges: the man who owned the Chevy dealership, the First Presbyterian Church Choir Director, and the beloved front desk lady at the YMCA. Sue Ann maintained her composure as she was quickly eliminated in the first rounds of both the evening gown and the swimsuit categories.

Sue Ann's mother and sister, Pat, embraced her backstage, and Pat poured out warm water and lemon from a Thermos. Her mother chaffed her cold hands and Pat whispered encouragement. A musical interlude sounded and the girl with a lit candle in her mouth who performed tricks with a jump rope skipped backstage. Another interlude followed the young lady who had clogged her way through the eighteenth-century tune "Ode to a Swan" as she clattered off stage.

"Sue Ann Worley," called the car dealer, and she glided onstage, graceful in her two-inch heels. The introduction to her song was cued, she lifted her eyes over the audience and swept into the first line: "So many nights I'd sit by my window . . ." Her voice was strong and melodious and sure, and she finished full-throated and confident on "You light up my life." She humbly dropped into a deep curtsy.

There was a breathless pause in the auditorium, then sporadic "Oh mys" and "Wows" and "Did you knows?" popped out here and there. They swelled into applause, and a roar of amazement and approval rolled through the hall."Encore! More! More!." Even the judges leaped to their feet.

Sue Ann looked to them. They nodded vigorously, smiling. She sang a slow, rich, a capella "Amazing Grace," each stanza stepping up a half-note.

Well, what do you think? Sue Ann swept the judges' votes and walked away with the crown of the 1998 Pancake Princess that night.

She entered the Curtis Institute of Music on full scholarship the following September. She had nineteen letters of recommendation to the famous Ohio Conservatory. I lost track of her after that. Her family did not come out of Rocky Pine Valley very often, and folks largely forgot about the little songstress. Sister Pat told her inquiring customers only that Sue Ann was doing well up north. Her clientele did not ask after that.

I am on an email list for certain cultural events around the world. A notification from the Royal Albert Hall in London popped up in December of 2014.

And there was Sue Ann—Susanna Worley—gowned in sumptuous garnet velvet. Her once-lank hair was sculpted into rich blond waves, framing a face no longer gaunt, but full and beautiful. A warm gaze of composure had replaced the eager hungry look in her eyes.

She was the soprano lead, Dona Elvira, in Mozart's *Don Giovanni*, backed by the London Philharmonic. Proud and smiling, I wrote "First Place, Princess" with my finger across the computer screen.

Sue Ann's mother had passed on, but I drove out to Rocky Pine Valley the following month, picked up Pat and we jetted across the Big Pond. Thrilled to our fingertips, we reveled in Sue Ann's, I mean Susanna's, performance. As the second standing ovation melted away and opera goers were leaving the hall, Susanna came out from behind the curtain to introduce Michael, first chair in the violin section of the Philharmonic and her husband. Then her nanny brought out little Alexandra, her three-year-old daughter. The next four wonderful days were spent with Susanna, Michael, and Alexandra in their London townhouse and touring the bucolic Lake District with them. We agreed that the Pancake Princess had grasped her dream, and with perseverance, talent, and sheer faith, was scaling the heights of her profession.

Brava, Princessa!

WAMPUS CAT

I was down at Chestoa on the Nolichucky River one June night, camping with my friends. We pulled our van in, set up camp, rolled out our bags, and went swimming in the river. Even in the summer, the Nolichucky is one cold river, about fifty degrees, fed by cold creeks. We cooked a supper of fried taters, onions, and sausages over the fire and swapped some tall tales over hot chocolate until about eleven.

We had just crawled, relaxed and happy, into our sleeping bags when Jim heard a loud rustling in the laurel thicket behind us.

"Wha-what was th-that, Danny?" asked Terry as she sat up in her blankets.

"Aww, that's nothing—just a possum ambling along looking for some left-overs."

"It's got big yellow eyes for a 'nothing.'"

We all looked in the direction she was pointing, and our mouths gaped open. About five feet up in the laurel was a pair of big, cat-like, slanted eyes—yellow as a summer gourd and glaring with malevolence!

Jim said, "That's too big for a house cat and too big for a bobcat—a bobcat's too shy and wouldn't come around our fire anyway."

We stared into the dark, trying to figure out what the creature was. The unblinking eyes shifted to the left to an opening in the laurel, and we saw—this huge dark gray cat with a stripey hide and a long swishy tail. It opened its mouth and the fire glinted on long, ivory canine teeth. It lowered its head as a guttural sound somewhere between a snarl and a hiss surged through its red lips—red like blood.

And we knew at once—WE were the leftovers!

But that was not all . . .

It was standing on its hind legs and it was over five feet tall!

Jim hollered, "Oh golly. Oh golly, it's a Wampus Cat!"

In a flash, the four of us were out of our bags, scrambling across the clearing and into the van, punching down the locks, panting in fear. Our heads swung as one back towards the laurel to see the cat walking into the clearing—still on its hind legs. It stalked toward our bags crushed on the ground and around our fire unafraid, then toward the van, growling and sniffing us, its long black whiskers quivering through dripping saliva.

Oh no! Could the beast breach the van?

Danny reached for his rifle and brandished it through the window. It turned away, and with a hateful look over its shoulder, the monster dropped to all fours. With a painter-like caterwauling shriek, it bounded up the riverside toward Lost Cove.

We spent the rest of the night huddled and shivering in the van, terrified the creature would return. At first light we crept out, collected our things, and we were gone.

Jim and Danny and Terry and I heard the Wampus Cat had been seen in the streets of Johnson City late at night. We haven't gone there after dark since, and we have not been back to Chestoa either. YOU had better stay away too!

REUBEN MAY

Reuben May grew up hard in the Southwest Virginia hill country—coal country. His father was a miner, as his father was before him. They lived in the Higgy Creek township that belonged to the Black Rock Coal and Coke Company. Their gray, weathered house was constructed of the cheapest raw materials: unfinished sawmill laps, tarpaper, and crumbling asphalt shingles. Old newspapers covered the walls of the three inside rooms and kept out some of the winter winds. An outhouse reposed in the farthest corner of the lot, adjacent to Higgy Creek. The land the coal company houses sat on was contaminated by run-off from the mine tailings. Higgy had turned a poisonous yellow-rust color, and all creek life had long since expired. Even the few scraggly trees and shrubs were yellow. Yellow and rust and gray were the colors of Reuben's life. A dense coal miasma, a kind of fog, filled the air day and night as the coke ovens smoked on. The days were filled with the rattle of the coal tipple and the sound of steam engines pulling in and leaving.

Reuben shared the little house with his two sisters and three brothers, mother Maryanne and father Sam Bob. He knew the mine beckoned to him and his younger brothers. He could feel it: accidents, maiming, black lung disease, over-burden collapses, death. Some of his schoolmates had already left for mines Number Two and Number Four by age fourteen. But at twelve he had a few years left.

Almost nightly he heard his mother begging his father, "There must be another way. Please, please, don't let them go down."

She mourned for the very fact that the four of them had been born male. Sam Bob mumbled the boys would earn money for the household, at least until they married and moved out. The two daughters would marry at fourteen or fifteen and go on their way. Children had to grow up fast in the mountains.

Reuben was a listener at the door. He heard his parents' discussions and his own future troubled him. He also did not want to go down and he wracked his brain searching for alternatives. If only his family had some land he might farm.

Each morning, he walked out of the dark cove to the school in town. He passed Mr. Harmon's fenced, sunlit vegetable plots and his pastures of fat, sleek cattle. His mouth watered for the fresh vegetables and the beef on the hoof. His family's meals consisted of canned goods, dried beans, and salt pork traded in script at the Black Rock company store and tallied against Sam Bob's weekly earnings. His mother's attempts at raising cabbage and tomatoes in the back yard failed, as the little seedlings turned yellow, then brown, and dried up. The only thing the land produced at Higgy was dug from underground.

Over the course of his short life, Reuben had developed a conversational relationship with Mr. Harmon. Mr. Harmon had no children and he enjoyed talking with the eager, skinny child. *That boy's got some gumption. Most unusual,* he thought, as they discussed the life cycle of the crops Mr. Harmon had planted. Reuben absorbed farm knowledge like the sour land absorbed the rain. If only he had some land. He longed to see the earth bring forth food! He longed to grow it and to eat it!

Mr. Harmon saw how Reuben looked longingly at the maturing vegetables. One afternoon, they were hanging on the fence talking, and Mr. Harmon asked if the boy wanted some cabbage and squash (the tomatoes, beans, and corn were not ready).

"Oh yes! But I don't have any money."

"Well, what have ye got to trade?"

Reuben searched his pockets and came up with his comb, harmonica, and blue aggie, a beautiful marble won at the schoolyard recess. He thought long and hard. He had won the aggie after shooting with great consideration and focus for two months, playing marbles not as desirable until he captured the prized blue aggie. But he kept seeing his mother's face when he brought home the vegetables.

"All righty," he agreed.

"Oh, it's blue and a fine one," said Mr. Harmon, rolling it around in his palm. "But I really like the green ones better."

"I can get ye a green one. It might take some time, but I'll get a green one." Reuben was suddenly afraid of losing the cabbage and squash.

"Well, ye take this poke and bring me a green one when ye get it." Mr. Harmon pocketed the blue aggie. He handed over a flour sack of vegetables.

Reuben ran home with his prize. He didn't think it odd that Mr. Harmon liked marbles. He didn't think it odd at all.

The family slurped up the fried squash, boiled cabbage and salt pork for supper, and there was a lot left over too. Sam Bob insisted Reuben had stolen the vegetables and the sheriff would be coming any time. He threatened to wear him out!

Reuben explained the price for the vegetables was his blue aggie and that Mr. Harmon wanted a green one. "I'll get a green aggie too, and more vegetables!" he promised the family.

"But look at this, here's yer blue marble," said his mother, turning the flour sack inside out. "It's jes' like Joseph's brothers found the gold cup in Benjamin's grain sack when they went down to Egypt to buy food. Ye'll have to take Mr. Harmon's marble back to him."

"Aha!" shouted Sam Bob. He ripped off his belt and charged at Reuben, who fled out the door.

It took Reuben three weeks to earn a green marble at shoot-out. He had fresh intentions now. He passed Mr. Harmon's vegetable patch morning and afternoon, looking yearningly at the pole beans on their trellises getting longer and fuller by the day, but the farmer was not there. On Friday afternoon, finally, Mr. Harmon was at the fence and smiled as Reuben came down the road.

"See here, Mr. Harmon, here's yer blue marble I paid you."

"Well, I told ye I liked green ones better. Do ye have one today?" Mr. Harmon smiled broadly at the eager boy.

"Jes' so happens I do," said Reuben, pulling it proudly from his pocket.

"Well, that will do fer some green beans and taters." Mr. Harmon pulled a folded flour sack from his pocket. Mr. Harmon forked up the new potatoes while Reuben pulled the beans one by one, careful not to rip the vines. Mr. Harmon watched approvingly, and then loaded up the sack with potatoes and green beans, accepting Reuben's green marble. They conversed a good long time about Japanese beetles on the beans and potato beetles and what could be done to control those pests. Mr. Harmon was pleased with how Reuben absorbed anything and everything about the crops. He asked what the boy would do about tomato hornworms.

"I think when ye see that the caterpillar's eatin' the leaves so fast, it's too late. It'll strip the plant by the afternoon. Ye got to get out early in the morning and look for where the butterfly laid her eggs and get 'em off afore they hatch into caterpillars."

Mr. Harmon approved of this strategy and told Reuben he had good ideas. Then he said thoughtfully, "Ye know, I really like them red marbles."

When Reuben got home, there was the green marble hiding amongst the green beans. "I don't understand," he said to himself, "but I'll see if I can win a red marble, red like ripe tomaters. They're awful dear."

That next Monday at recess, Reuben won the coveted red marble off Jenks Sizemore and he ran to Mr. Harmon's vegetable patch after school. Mr. Harmon stood there smiling at him. He already had a large flour sack of ripe tomatoes waiting, some for supper, some to juice, some to lay up on the window ledge, and plenty to can. "A red marble's worth all these," Mr. Harmon said as he pocketed the marble. "Tell me, Reuben, could ye work with me this summer? I'm expanding my vegetable plots and could really use yer help breaking the new ground and getting it ready to plant next spring. I'll pay ye good and give ye vegetables."

Why, Reuben did not even have to think about it. "Oh yes! Thanky, yes."

They worked together all summer, breaking new ground, harvesting vegetables, and loading the trucks that came to haul the vegetables to the big city. Reuben made folding money and took home vegetables. Come fall, he had cabbage, onions, turnip and mustard greens, and the last of the tomatoes to bring home, and big-leaved, blue-green collards waiting for the first freeze to mellow. His mother and sisters were kept busy preparing and canning the vegetables for the winter. He even experimented with fall broccoli, which looked like little trees. He had neither seen nor tasted that before. He was becoming quite skilled in the garden under Mr. Harmon's tutelage, and the proceeds made life so much easier for his family. One July afternoon, a big, old truck with high board sides pulled into Mr. Harmon's barnyard. Several of the cattle were herded up the plank into the truck, and it pulled off.

"They're going to the auction and that big ole steer's going to the butcher," he said. "Ye come back after supper and there will be a surprise for ye."

When Reuben returned, there were twenty-five pounds of fresh beef portioned, rolled up in brown butcher's paper, and tied with string.

"This here's for yer Mama. Tell her yer the best worker I've ever had and the smartest boy I've ever seen, and I'll see ye tomorrow morning bright and early."

But Mr. Harmon did not see Reuben the next morning or any other morning for that good man had a fatal heart attack during the night.

His death did not end their collaboration however, for Mr. Harmon, without heirs, had left the ten-acre vegetable garden, the house, the barn, the livestock, the woodlot, and over one-hundred acres of prime pastureland to twelve-year-old Reuben May, who now had a life above ground. In time, Reuben employed his brothers as he expanded the farm and its holdings. And he was forever grateful to his mentor and benefactor, the kind Mr. Harmon.

Today, May-Harmon Farm trucks bearing the tagline, "Farm-Fresh Produce and USDA Grade Prime Beef", proudly grown in Higgy Creek, Virginia can be seen making their deliveries all over Southwest Virginia, East Tennessee, and Northeast Kentucky.

Oh, and on the morning the will was read, the estate lawyer handed Reuben a red marble.

THE PACKHORSE LIBRARY INITIATIVE

Lou Powers wondered what sort of meeting was being held down at the Pikeville Library. It was 1932 and the heart of the Great Depression in Kentucky. Her husband had been laid off from the local coal mining company, and things at home were tight—real tight. She went inside and found a seat among ten other women from the community. She saw her cousin, Flora, and older married sister, Pearly.

A man she did not know came out dressed up in city finery and said, "The president up in Washington DC is very concerned about unemployment and illiteracy—that's folks who can't read—and he's started a program called the Pack Horse Library. He wants to hire you ladies who have a horse or mule to ride out to the far-off cabins and take books to 'em." He went on to describe a forty-hour work week for which they would be paid five dollars. The ladies looked at each other in wonder: five whole dollars! How hard could it be?

Lou found out how hard it was as she rode upwards of one hundred miles a week. She steered her mare across creeks and mud flats, through deep snow and trackless forests.

After the first week, she rode home on Friday evening and told her husband, "Joe, I got to borry yore pants. I cain't sit a horse in a dress."

Laughing, he handed her his mine pants. "You might as well, I ain't wearing 'em."

Lou found herself calling on the town folks, asking them for old newspapers, magazines, and stained, dog-eared books. "We gotter build up our library," she said. "I give out two or three books at each one of my stops."

On Saturdays, Lou, Pearly, and Cousin Flora sat around Lou's kitchen table cutting up magazines and papers. They pasted the articles and pictures into scrapbooks with flour and water paste. The scrapbooks made up for the printed material that was lacking.

The cabin women requested, "Give us some words on sewin' and makin' crafts and puttin' up food." They got the scrapbooks.

"No, go on, now, we ain't innerested."

Words flung across a stream from a front porch. Lou figured out the adults were embarrassed—they couldn't read. The next time she was by, she sidled up to the porch before she hallooed and offered to read to the children while the mama fixed supper. She stayed to eat, and after supper, continued to read to a now-rapt group of adults.

"Gimme that thang," said the old Granny. "I learnt to read from the Good Book."

Lou slipped out for home.

During the three years she was a pack horse librarian, she had many adventures on her routes. There was the time a rattlesnake spooked her horse and it dumped her into the road and took off. Another time, wild hogs charged out of the woods and her mare took her for a wild ride. Once she was lost in a blizzard trying to get home and almost froze to death. Riding over Pine Mountain one evening, three men staggered out of the rhododendron and tried to grab her reins. Still, she was determined to get the books in her saddle-bags and basket hampers through to the most isolated cabins and farms. Many friendships were made with women in the outback hungry for connection and conversation.

The Pack Horse Library was defunded in 1943 after wartime ended unemployment, and Joe went back to work. Lou was among the one thousand women who rode mountain trails, bringing a taste of the outside world to families in twenty-nine mountain counties of Kentucky, Tennessee, and the Virginias. These were the foundational years of many counties' public libraries, the joy of reading, and the encouragement of schoolchildren.

Lou's granddaughter, Barbara, followed in her footsteps by also serving in a mobile book service in the 1950s—she drove the Bookmobile.

CLOUDLAND

In 1780, iron ore was discovered at a dot on the map called Cranberry, North Carolina. You can find that dot in Watauga County on the very Northwestern border of the state.

At this same time, a railroad was being proposed with a terminus either in Elizabethton or ten miles south in Johnson City, Tennessee. It was about thirty miles from Johnson City to Cranberry through the Doe River Gorge, very narrowly situated between Cedar and Fork Mountains. There was precious little room for a railroad, even a narrow gauge with three-foot-wide tracks. Finally, after thirty years of slow bond floats, laborious grubbing through the unforgiving gorge, the Civil War years, and financial high jinks, the Eastern Tennessee and Western North Carolina narrow gauge railroad was finished in 1882. There were several charcoal/coke ovens and a forge in Cranberry using the output of iron ore mined there. The train was eventually extended to Boone, North Carolina. It was said that no one came in or went out of Boone until the train came.

About the same time, Northerners interested in making money from Appalachian resources of timber and coal, were buying up the mountains. Former Union General John Wilder from Indiana acquired 7,000 acres of the Roan Mountain summit and surrounding areas, straddling the Tennessee-North Carolina line. He built two hotels on the Roan. The first, rather primitive one, burned down. The second hotel was called Cloudland as seventy-five percent of the time it was socked in by clouds and fog. It was state of the art in 1885 with 166 bedrooms And strangely enough, just one bathroom. Seven states and 100 mountain peaks could be seen from the verandas when the weather permitted. At over 6200 feet, it was the highest hotel east of the Rockies. Wealthy international guests traveled to stay there. Among the notables were naturalists Andre Michaux, Asa Gray, and John Muir. The chief draws were the clear, hay-fever-free air, the absence of mosquitoes and snakes and, of course, the natural gardens of magnificent pink and white rhododendrons.

The following story is from the journal of a young visitor to Cloudland.

"My name is Caroline Vandergriff and I was born and raised in Baltimore, Maryland. Young people of my age and social status would take long trips around the country and the Grand Tour to Europe upon graduation. Several of my classmates and our mothers began this odyssey in August, 1894, by taking the train from Baltimore to Johnson City, Tennessee. We had read about this huge hotel built on top of the world called Cloudland. We were eager to see it. I had never been outside of Maryland and had not seen mountains before, although I had read about the jungles of the Appalachians covered in old growth trees. Terrible wildcats and bears and venomous snakes lived there. I set out on this trip excited and scared at the same time!

"We boarded this little train in Johnson City. I call it little because it was very narrow. We chugged along and passed through five tunnels cut from the living rock and a terrifying gorge where the tracks plunged down into a canyon with high walls and a river running far below the narrow track clearance. I think we all unconsciously leaned as one toward the cliff side. Disembarking at the tiny Roan Mountain station, we climbed aboard a rough-looking four-horse hack driven by a real mountain man. His name was Sherman Pippin, obviously named for a mountain apple. He was of medium height, broad-shouldered, with glossy chestnut hair and the bluest eyes. Oh my. Now, mind you, this description is just for the journal Mother is having me keep on the trip.

"The hack ride was described in the hotel literature as 'An exhilarating twelve-and-a-half mile ride up to Cloudland.' Rather than exhilarating, it was terrifying. The wagon swayed this way and that on the narrow road. The horses seemed barely able to pull the wagon, making me think we were suddenly going to lose purchase and fly backwards to an unknown fate. We hung on for dear life! But that was not all. The road was hot and dusty, and we were dying of thirst. The trip up the mountain seemed to take hours and hours. Our complaining grew louder.

"Sherman finally pulled the wagon over. A small keg had been loaded onto the wagon with us and our luggage. He took out his penknife, bored a little hole in the side, brought the potation around, and held it up for us to drink. Rather than refreshing water, it was Tennessee whiskey, bound for the hotel's bar! Mother demurred, but finally took a sip, and then a long drink. I say, modestly, that we all took several drinks and slaked our thirst. When we were satisfied, Sherman cut a little plug from a stick of wood and fitted it to the hole so the bartender would not know differently. He and his passengers, or I should say, his patrons, arrived on the mountain in exceptionally good humor—jolly, gay, and well-watered. We could remain in that state as long as we drank on the Carter County, Tennessee, side. The state line was painted white and ran down the length of the dining room table. Imbibing on the Mitchell County, North Carolina, side could get you imprisoned in the local pokey, as they called it. We thoroughly enjoyed our stay at Cloudland and returned home by the precarious route we had come with stories of the primitive and wild Tennessee mountains."

There are other notorious stories of Sherman Pippin, who later became an engineer on the ET and WNC railroad, and many about the train itself, which officially ceased operations in October 1950. But its best story still takes place every day for the hundreds of thousands of joyful people who ride "Tweetsie" on its track between Blowing Rock and Boone, North Carolina.

THE VEGETABLE MISTRESS

The idea for this story was shared by my friend and colleague Trish Taylor in 2018 in Franklin, North Carolina. I developed the story with her permission.

Mr. Jackson was married, and my mother was a widow of nineteen years, circumspect and chaste in her solitude.

They had grown up on the same street, tumbled through school together, vied for 4-H ribbons in agronomy and horticulture, and married each other's best friends. They joked about being double first cousins.

Birthday and anniversary celebrations, beach vacations, endless schedules of children's events, Friday night potluck dinners, and Canasta card parties ran like silken threads through the years, tying the couples' lives together. When the four of them were spoken of, their names were always said together, like conjoined twins.

My mother sang her way through our bath times, while making meals, and on Sunday afternoon strolls hand-in-hand with Dad through the neighborhood. She thriftily preserved her garden produce with a smile and whistled under her breath as she did up our snowsuits. Such a cheerful household we grew up in. Mother and her childhood friend, Mrs. Jackson, talked two or three times a day on the phone and visited over the backyard fence bright with purple wisteria, fuchsia clematis, and huge white moonflowers. The two properties adjoined like our lives to theirs.

My father, a World War II veteran and prisoner of war camp survivor, suffered with bouts of debilitating anxiety and depression. Mr. Jackson took him fly-fishing to calm and encourage him. They spent Saturday mornings on the Davidson River. One silently crept up the river casting and the other fly-fished downstream. They sat upon the large rocks that bounded the river, their feet dangling just inches above the rushing water, and ate a fisherman's lunch: Vienna Sausages, saltine crackers and Coca-Colas. Mother and Mrs. Jackson took turns adding homemade cookies or brownies to the lunch pokes. My father breathed slowly, rhythmically, in the fresh air and relaxed within the harmony of sun-spangled water, green vines trailing down the rhododendron banks, and the lightning flash of rainbow trout in and out of the shadows that only fishermen know. Mrs. Jackson taught Dad's restless hands to crochet and make hooked woolen rugs.

Mother and Mr. Jackson fought friendly battles over the girth of their pumpkins and the crispness of their pickles each year at the Macon County Fair.

Mr. Jackson would say, "My patty pan squash is plumper than yours, and my greasy beans are longer and shinier."

Mother, arms akimbo, would counter with, "Humph! My heirloom tomatoes are heavier and darker and my ford hook limas more perfect than yours."

And on and on the competition went.

My siblings and the Jacksons' son and daughter finished school at Western Carolina University and North Carolina State. They moved away, found jobs and spouses, and left home for good. They were mountain folks, so they moved to the mountains: one to the Cascade Range, another to the Colorado Rockies, and one to the White Mountains of New Hampshire. My brother, truly the adventurous one, crossed the Big Pond to the Pennines of England. I alone remained in town with my husband and our son.

Slowly, imperceptibly at first, then gathering a painful, bewildering speed, dementia overtook Mrs. Jackson, and the precious relationship with my mother slipped away. The magic circle was broken when my father died following a long battle with cancer.

It was the two of them now, my mother and Mr. Jackson. They would sit at her kitchen table in the late afternoons, drinking coffee and sometimes a small glass of garnet-colored merlot. There was not much conversation, not much laughter any longer. All that had been said. But there was a pure intimacy born of decades' knowledge of habits, preferences, and idio-syncrasies—a lovely acceptance nourished by shared joys and sorrows.

His entrée to her kitchen was always a peach basket of produce from his garden. In early spring, emerald snow peas emerged from a collection of colorful satiny lettuces punctuated by round rosy radishes and star-tling white daikons. Summertime brought the basket overflowing with crimson beefsteak tomatoes, stal-wart ears of golden corn napped with silvery silks, and green snap beans. Crisp Jonathan apples appeared in early fall, followed by cabbages and turnip greens kissed by frosty nights. His root cellar brought forth winter-stored Kennebeck potatoes and hardy squash. Sometimes just a single perfect peach on a cobalt-blue plate or a large handful of dark green collards tied with a red string bow. His offerings sat atop the table between Mr. Jackson and my mother. Looking up out of soft eyes, she smiled her thanks.

Their friendship had endured so many years—all the way back to Mama May's Nursery School.

At the close of day, I came by unannounced to check on Mother and found Mr. Jackson in his usual spot at the table. A gentle smile of quiet presence creased his old face. The small basket of cucumbers, his tribute, sat before her. A last beam of sunshine pierced the lace at the kitchen window and created a nimbus of sparkling gold about her silver head.

He rose, and without a glance in my direction, bent tenderly over my mother's hand, his eyes lifting slowly to hers. Their white hair, lined faces, and trembling hands all fell away. In that one look, I saw the identity that had sustained and glorified my mother for almost twenty years—perhaps many more.

I saw him.

I saw her.

The ninety-year-old Vegetable Mistress.

MR. BURNS

A statue stands in the town square of Burnsville, North Carolina, honoring a naval hero of the war of 1812, 360 miles from the coast. Otway Burns never set foot in Western North Carolina; he never wore a uniform; he never served in the American Armed Forces.

He did serve his state and country for sixty of his seventy-five years, a long and illustrious career cut short by doing the right thing—serving a purpose that benefitted the many, not the individual. His was a life of notable triumphs and disheartening disappointments.

Otway Burns was born two miles from Swansboro in Onslow County, North Carolina, on Queen's Creek in 1775. He was a second-generation American, descended from Scottish immigrants who had come to America in 1734 from Glasgow. His father, Frances Burns, and grandfather, also Frances Burns, maintained an interest in maritime affairs in Swansboro. Growing up working on his father's farm on the creek close to the Bogue Inlet and the Atlantic Ocean, Otway developed a love of fishing and the sea early in life. He went to sea at age fourteen, working his way up through various duty-defined positions to master merchantman and merchant captain. By age thirty-five, Otway was the captain of his own vessel, in partnership with Edward Pasteur, a New Bern physician, planter, and politician. They sailed a small coastal trader that ranged as far north as Maine. How happy he must have been, following his love of the sea.

He married his first wife and cousin, Joanna Grant, at age thirty-four in 1809. They resided in Swansboro where his only child, Owen Burns, was born in 1810. In 1813 Joanna left Otway, taking Owen with her. For the next five years, Owen lived with one maternal relative after another. Otway won a custody suit in court. It cost him $1000, but he finally had his son with him. A waiver of liability was posted publicly in January, 1814, that read Otway would no longer be responsible for his wife and her debts. Joanna died suddenly that September.

Four months after Joanna passed, Otway married Jane Hall from Beaufort, a young lady purported to be between eighteen and twenty years old. There are indications that she was the love of his life. He built a grand house for her in Beaufort, and they were separated only by her death in 1842. They had no children. Jane's relationship with her husband's son Owen was not an easy one; he became more angry with her as time went on, and at one point, refused to talk to her at all. One can imagine that a child's unsophisticated understanding had problems with his mother Joanna's separation from his father, being passed around his mother's family for five years, and his father's taking a new younger wife so soon after his mother's death.

This brings us to 1812 and what is known as the Second War for Independence. The last major conflict with England, it reaffirmed American independence and solidified the country's position on the world stage. The British navy was impressing American sailors on the High Seas, forcing men into military and naval forces by compulsion and blocking American trade routes with France. Britain's war with France had depleted her military reserves, and young, seasoned American seamen were snatched by raiding British frigates and Men of War. The British caused trouble on the frontier by fomenting Indian attacks on settlers. For the first time in American history, the country declared war on a foreign power.

Otway Burns was an American patriot and resisted the British blockade of southern ports that threatened his livelihood and his country's autonomy. He and Dr. Pasteur were on their coastal trader in Portland, Maine, when he learned the United States had declared war on Great Britain. They sailed straightway to New York City, where they looked at several ships. They located a schooner, *Zephyr*, built in the West River Shipyards in Maryland in 1808 and purchased it for $8,000. They sold shares to businessmen in southeastern North Carolina for $260 to help finance their purchase. There has been some speculation about the true identity of the ship; it might have been the *Le Vere*, which had similar measurements: 85.5 feet long, a beam of 12.5 feet, draft of 8.67 feet, and weight of 147.42 tons. However, it has been confirmed as the *Zephyr*, as no ship registers exist in New York confirming the *LeVere's* presence. To approximate size, the USS Frigate *Constitution* was over twice as large.

Zephyr was a fine, sleek ship, and the owner allowed Otway to sail her up the Hudson River before the purchase. He renamed the ship *Snap Dragon,* as it was very quick and maneuverable, carrying six to eight guns: one or two twelve-pound pivot guns, five to six carriage guns, plus a large array of small arms: pistols, muskets, pickaxes, blunderbusses, swords, cutlasses, and boarding pikes.

During the war, the United States Navy was seriously undermanned and fairly ineffective. At the beginning of the war, Great Britain had 800 ships equipped for fighting out of 1060 under sail, while the United States could send out only seventeen seaworthy ships out of twenty under sail. The largest of the American fleet were the *Constitution, The President,* and the *Independence.* Owners of merchantmen refitted their ships or sold and bought others. They exchanged trade use for privateering, which was a logical move.

The legality of privateering was recognized in the US Constitution. Article 1, Section 8, Clause 11 empowered Congress to issue "Letters of Marque and Reprisal." This was a license that allowed private citizens to attack enemy ships and confiscate their cargoes, crew, and the ship itself. On occasion, if the ship was not sea-worthy following battle or had no valuable cargo, the crew members were removed and the ship burned. Every member of a privateer crew took an oath of compliance to the nation's rules and practices. This was the difference between privateering and piracy; the oath specified a single target nation, not a piratical attacking of ships at will. There were many benefits to the issuing government: It was a way for governments to disrupt an enemy's war effort, to fund the war, and to fight their wars using mercenaries rather than their own navies. This was ideal for the United States, owing to the aforementioned description of paltry ship inventory. Letters of Marque were issued during the War of 1812 to hundreds of American ship owners who captured over 2500 British merchant ships and seriously damaged British trade. This number does not include the British ships of war destroyed or taken captive by American ships to be refitted and sent back into combat against English ships.

Privateering originated in the Middle Ages and continued until forty-five nations signed the Declaration of Paris in 1856, effectively ending it. Three countries with small navies, including the United States, abstained. However, the American government has not issued any Letters of Marque and Reprisal since the mid-nineteenth century. Piracy on the high seas continues today in areas of the world such as the Gulf of Guinea, encompassing the coasts of Gabon to Liberia, the Somalian coast, Southeast Asia, and the Indian Ocean.

Privateering is an interesting concept and a "cousin" to the illegal practice of piracy. It depended upon whether you were the predator nation or the prey. At the time of the War of 1812, the laws of nations recognized privateering as legitimate. *Snap Dragon* received Letters of Marque on August 27, 1812. However, the "good men" of New Bern were concerned that privateering was the same as piracy and contrived to stop Otway, whom they labelled "That Licensed Robber." Local officials used legal and non-legal means to interfere with his recruiting efforts. Recruited crew members were arrested and imprisoned for indebtedness, having been seduced with liberal "loans" of paltry amounts as small as three dollars. A boatload of six constables rowed out to the *Snap Dragon,* which was anchored offshore, and attempted to serve Captain Burns with warrants, but his crew capsized the boat and left lawmen swimming for it. A town attorney, Frances Xavier Martin, made several scurrilous remarks about Otway, who rowed to shore, apprehended the councilor in a public house, and tossed him into the Neuse River. Otway completed his crew in Norfolk, Virginia, where he met another privateer, the *Revenge,* and they agreed to sail together. After tacking for eight to ten days, Otway determined the Captain of the *Revenge* "sailed too slowly," and they parted ways.

On October 14, 1812, the trim and speedy *Snap Dragon* carrying twenty-five officers and men set sail from New Bern to intercept British-flagged shipping. Only six to ten sailors were required to man a ship of the *Snap Dragon's* size; the extra crew were prize captains, prize masters and lieutenants. They would sail the captured ship, crew, and cargo (the "prize") back to Southport, Swansboro, or New Bern, enabling the *Snap Dragon* to continue on. Also on the crew list were seasoned fighters whose job was to board and overwhelm enemy ships' sailors. Men on land in Otway's employ sold the captured cargo after "prize courts" determined the qualifications of a vessel as a prize. The money obtained from the sales were divided up by a pre-determined and agreed-upon amount. There were levies placed on the values of the cargo and the captured ships. Import duties were owed to the government when the spoils were sold. Two percent of the sales went to the customs collector and into a government fund to support the widows and orphans of seamen killed in battle and disabled seamen. Usually, the owners received half and the crew took half after these levies. These proportions made Otway a fabulously wealthy man, as he received portions as both owner and crew (captain). His proceeds from twenty months of privateering as captain have been estimated at $4,000,000. Such a fortune! He was said to have a "sailor's luck." "He was impetuous and brave to a fault and always correct in instincts and when to force action and when the British were attempting to decoy him into a trap."

During his maiden voyage, Otway took nine prizes and several other smaller captures as he ranged from Norfolk to Curacao, a Dutch Caribbean island about sixty-five kilometers north of Venezuela. The *Snap Dragon* became the "Terror of British merchant ships from Greenland to Brazil." British merchant traffic was heavy in the West Indies. He inflicted so much damage, the British government offered $50,000 reward for his capture, dead or alive. There would be no more recruitment trouble following the first voyage. Men came begging to be enlisted in the service of the *Snap Dragon*. Captain Otway never lost a ship or a cargo, and crew members could make $3000 from one prize. Merchants waited for him to take their goods, and many paid very well, above the usual charge.

The second voyage of the *Snap Dragon,* from June 3, 1813, to August 16, 1813, was even more profitable than the first voyage. Believing the British Men of War were expecting him in the Caribbean, he turned north to Newfoundland. Otway secured nine more prizes, including the famed *HMS Brig Ann* with a cargo value of $368,520. Some sources suggested her value was closer to half a million. The gigantic haul required two days to transfer to the *Snap Dragon*. Four additional captured vessels with their cargoes were steered to American ports by Burns' prize captains and valued at more than $2.5 million.

His third and last voyage as captain returned him to the Caribbean. He took only one prize. It seemed his luck had turned. He was met by the British Letter of Marque *HMS Liverpool* carrying twenty-two guns. It rammed and damaged *Snap Dragon*, requiring Otway to seek temporary repairs in Venezuela and return to New Bern.

In his twenty months as captain of *Snap Dragon,* "He captured forty-two English vessels and cargo valued at greater than four million dollars. He made Prisoners of War of over three hundred English officers and sailors and gave successful battle to several of the enemy's war craft—a record of astounding audacity and brilliant success that has few parallels." He was considered the "pre-eminent privateer of the War of 1812." The *Snap Dragon's* actions prevented the British from unloading troops and supplies on American shores, which greatly aided the country.

So, with this record and recognition, why did he retire from active privateering? There may be four reasons. After the third voyage and the close call with the *HMS Liverpool,* he may have become unsure of his personal safety. Of about 100,000 men in the American naval labor pool, an estimated 14,000 officers and seamen were captured and imprisoned in the period of 1812 to 1815. Those taken were kept in less-than-desirable conditions while awaiting prisoner exchange. Both British and American prisoners were treated well by some captains and prison officers and very poorly by others. Officers and seamen taken captive by the British were either imprisoned in the cold, clammy Halifax prison on Melville Island, Nova Scotia, transported to England where they languished in prison barges off Plymouth, or relegated to the infamous Dartmore Prison located in County Devon. Many died from malnutrition, disease, and ill treatment. These were not outcomes of capture he would have relished. Otway was beginning to suffer from the "Sailor's Malady," rheumatism, which the chill conditions at sea exacerbated, and his reflexes might not have been as sure. Also during this voyage, his marriage to Joanna Grant began to come apart. Lastly, there were legal problems. Two similar allegations of the embezzlement of prize proceeds brought him into court within a year. It may be that his daring exploits and financial success had made him an object of jealousy; those who had opposed the recruitment of crew for the *Snap Dragon* had determined they now envied the proceeds of the outcome.

Otway relinquished the helm of the ship to his trusted lieutenant, William Graham, in May, 1814, on its fourth and last voyage. It was almost immediately captured by the more heavily armed *HMS Martin* off the coast of Nova Scotia. The British Men of War were the weaponized giants of their era, and the *Snap Dragon* was a smaller but usually more nimble ship than the cumbersome frigates. Mr. Graham did not, to the misfortune of the owners and the graceful ship, have the same seafaring abilities as Burns, and Dr. Pasteur had deemed himself too old and unsteady to take the ship to sea. There had been other problems also. Prize captains sometimes dishonestly took the captured ships to ports that Otway had not approved,or may not have been able to reach a non-blockaded port, and prizes were lost. The *Snap Dragon's* crew spent the remainder of the war in Dartmore Prison.

The *Snap Dragon* was bought by merchants in New Brunswick, Canada, who outfitted her as a British privateer, but she had lost her magic and was unsuccessful in raiding American merchants. Another set of Canadian merchants then purchased her, outfitted her as an island trader between Cuba and Jamaica, and the brave ship was lost at sea in 1814. This may or may not have been the schooner's outcome.

Otway Burns must have felt disappointment and sadness at the demise of his beautiful ship. However, he moved forward. He used his fortune to move into several entrepreneurial endeavors back in his home territory. In 1818, he established shipyards in Swansboro, where his bright and futuristic thinking led him to build the first steamship in North Carolina. He named it *Prometheus,* and it plied the Cape Fear River between Wilmington and Southport. He was once again in the trading business. He built a beautiful house in New Bern for his lovely bride, Jane Hall. One section of the house was constructed as a store that supplied farming and nautical supplies to everyone in the area; another section was opened as a taproom. New Bern was his new hometown, and he determined to make the most of the populace's every need.

Salt was at that time worth more than its weight in silver and gold. It was greatly in demand for salting down the produce of both sea and land and it was hard to come by. Boiling and evaporation were the tools of salt production. Otway used his own funds to recruit and train locals in the salt-making process. Eventually, over one hundred salt production companies were formed in Southeastern North Carolina, many owing to Otway's assistance. He owned several fishing vessels, and the salt works and the chandlery store were adjunct businesses that also supported the fishing enterprise.

In 1823, he built the large ship *Warrior,* and in 1831, *Henry,* using the sturdy live oaks found on the Shackelford and Bogue Banks. They carried cargo from North Carolina as far away as South Africa and the West Indies. Always an innovator, Otway also built a very fast two-masted sailboat—incorporating the first centerboard in its design in the region—for his personal use and named it *Snap Dragon*, in honor of the schooner that had brought him such great wealth. He bought a 365-acre plantation on the North River in Carteret County and, after the custom of the time, owned eleven slaves, some skilled workmen in his other enterprises.

His road took a new turn when his fame in the war and standing as a businessman led to politics. Beginning in 1821, he served seven terms in the North Carolina House of Representatives and four terms in the North Carolina Senate: eleven two-year terms representing the voters of Carteret County.

The US Army Corps of Engineers persuaded him to invest some of his war earnings in the construction of Fort Macon. This opportunity fit in line with his advocacy for improving agricultural and manufacturing industries. The fort was to be built on the Bogue Banks and would be the largest public works project in the Outer Banks until recent times. Otway built a large brick kiln, which he co-owned, and he financially supported four other brick-building businesses until they were established. He paid, again from his own funds for highly skilled brickmakers from up north to teach locals how to manufacture the building materials.

He always considered the welfare of the people around him. When the fort was completed, masons had used over four million of Burns' bricks. As he promoted economic development in his region, he aided in the construction of the turnpike from Fayetteville to Wilkesboro, improved the navigability of Cape Fear and Deep River, and obtained charters for railroads to be built throughout the state. He favored modernizing transportation routes to move products on land from area to area, just as he had on the High Seas. He modified his belief in slavery and spoke out in favor of freeing the slaves, supporting one proposal to protect freed slaves from discrimination and re-enslavement and another to allow slave owners to emancipate their own slaves. He favored the popular election of sheriffs and clerks of court rather than the appointment system that had supported cronyism.

Andrew Jackson, hero of the Battle of New Orleans at which he defeated the British during the war, and the president, was a close friend. Otway visited the White House on many occasions. Their commonality met in each man's belief in public welfare and in the greater good. Otway put his money where it advanced the well-being of the citizens of Southeastern North Carolina, but he also had visions for the entire state and beyond. The many long conversations he had with President Jackson must have influenced him, as well as his innate belief in fairness, for he was willing to act against the interests of the eastern part of the state, which had enjoyed disproportional representation in the legislature.

He supported the creation of new western counties: Yancey, Macon, Davidson, and Cherokee. On December 9,1833, the North Carolina Senate passed an act establishing Yancey County, to be formed from parts of Burke and Buncombe Counties. Senator Otway Burns cast the tie-breaking vote to form the new counties in Western North Carolina. Come the turn of the 1834 New Year, he was an outcast, a traitor to the eastern power magnate counties. His vote was opposed by ninety percent of his Cartaret County constituency. His perceived disloyalty to his region ended his political career. The ungrateful Easterners had decided to punish him for his willingness to single-handedly reduce their power in state government.

This brings us to the Town of Burnsville. The grateful Westerners honored Otway Burns by naming the county seat of newly birthed Yancey after him. During this time period, he began to suffer financial ruin. Some early biographies cited his open-handed spirit of generosity and there are certainly facts to support this. Others claimed poor management of his various businesses and the disappearing favor he had enjoyed as a political figure for twenty-two years. In reality, as happened to many others, he was probably a victim of over-extension and the economic downturn, which some rightfully term a depression, beginning in 1837.

Known as the Panic of 1837, it quickly spread world-wide and persisted for nearly seven years. It led to unemployment, bank failures, and collapses in commodities and property prices. Speculative lending practices in America, a collapsing land bubble, and a disastrous decline in cotton prices contributed to the economic disaster. President Jackson's fiscal policies were to blame. He did not extend the charter of the Bank of the United States and withdrew federal funds in the amount of approximately ten million dollars. This action left nobody to regulate fiscal matters, resulting in destabilization. High inflation resulted in eight hundred banks closing their doors, stifling economic growth and bankrupting numerous business.

Otway Burns was caught up in this economic chaos. He had borrowed heavily against his properties to finance his many business enterprises. He found himself over-extended and was forced to liquidate assets when creditors began insisting on repayment. Little by little, it all disappeared. He still had friends in the Jackson Administration, and they secured for him the sinecure of keeper of the Brant Shoal Island Lighthouse The lighthouse was near Portsmouth, where he moved in 1839. Shortly thereafter, his second wife, Jane Hall

Burns, died in 1839 at the age of sixty-seven, and in 1842, he was married for the third time to forty-eight-year-old Jane Smith, who also pre-deceased him. This might have been Otway's second love match, as this lady married him when he had nothing but the loneliness of the lighthouse. It sat out in the southern arm of Pamlico Sound on high stilts, no ingress from land save a rowboat.

By 1850, Otway was living with the family of John Hunter of Portsmouth. He appeared to be displaying "eccentricities" and may have been suffering with dementia. He died on October 25,1850, and was buried beside his second wife, Jane Hall Burns, in The Old Burying Ground graveyard in Beaufort.

An eighteen-pound cannon from the *Snap Dragon* surmounts his grave. Two communities in North Carolina have been named in his honor: a community east of Beaufort on the coast is named Otway, and, of course, the town and county seat of Yancey—Burnsville. But he may have been forgotten save for the efforts of his family, primarily Owen's son, Walter Frances Burns, and Owen's great-grandson, Walter Frances Burns III.

In 1909, a bronze statue of Otway Burns was erected on a granite pedestal in the town square of Burnsville. Thus began a love affair connecting the Otway Burns descendants to the Town of Burnsville. His grandson, Walter Frances Burns, son of Owen Burns of the

United States Navy, son of Captain Otway Burns, commissioned and paid for the statue. On the pedestal is a plaque that reads in part:

"He guarded well our seas,
Let our mountains honor him."

Originally, the statue's right hand held a sword and the left hand a bugle, apparent in the 1909 photograph. The dedication address was given by Walter Clark, Chief Justice of the Supreme Court of North Carolina. It was the first commemorative statue to be erected in North Carolina outside of Raleigh's Capital Square.

The first destroyer, *USS Burns,* was launched in 1918. Josephus Daniels was Secretary of the Navy and owner of the *Raleigh News and Observer.* The commander of the Atlantic Fleet objected and told Secretary Daniels, "There is not much difference between a privateer and a pirate."

Daniels replied, "In these days, there is not much difference between admirals and pirates in the twilight zone and since my association with admirals, I don't think there has been much change in a century and a half."

Apparently, the issue of privateers and pirates had not been resolved in some minds! The second destroyer, *USS Burns,* was built in the Charleson Shipyard in 1942 and served in the Pacific. It was Fletcher Class, armed with eight five-inch guns and sank a four-ship convoy of Japanese ships in the Marshall Islands. There is no record of any objections to her.

Great-great grandson Walter Frances Burns III of Maryland persuaded the State of North Carolina to honor Otway in 1983 with a statue erected in Swansboro. At great expense to himself, the statue was placed looking out to sea, a memorial to where Otway Burns' life as a seaman began.

The Burns family remains connected to the Navy with two descendants graduating from the Naval Academy and great-grandson Walter Burns serving on the World War Two destroyer.

The Yancey History Association in Burnsville is a small museum that contains an alcove dedicated to Captain Otway Burns. A copy of his portrait, the only known one, painted by F. Mahler hangs on the wall next to an 1812 flag and a handcrafted cherry wood table.

Great-great-grandson Walter Frances Burns III commissioned a replica of the *Snap Dragon* on a three-eighths-inch to one-foot scale in the 1990s. The Smithsonian Institute provided the plans, and Frank Shurick painstakingly constructed it over a year. When Mr. Burns decided to retire at age eighty and close his office in Florida where the ship sat, he began contacting museums and historical groups in the North Carolina lowcountry. No one was interested in displaying it. Someone suggested contacting the town of

Burnsville, which he did. President Chris Carter and Debbie Nance at the association were overjoyed to receive the model.

Mr. Burns had an appropriate shipping crate built to protect the ship, complete with figures of sailors and the captain. Guns and gun ports, various cargo articles, rigging, and sails completed the perfect little ship. Dissatisfied with commercial shipping arrangements, he hired a van and, accompanied by a friend, transported the *Snap Dragon* up to Burnsville. Included in the gift was the handmade cherry wood table, each leg containing sixteen different screws that were dismantled for travel, the model itself, and a custom-made glass display cabinet. Two days were required to reconstruct the table , put the model back together, and set up the cabinet. Mr. Burns was given the honor of placing the *Snap Dragon* inside the glass cabinet and was feted during his three day stay by town officials. Several articles were printed in area newspapers describing the event.

Burnsville and Yancey County residents still honor Captain Otway Burns today. High school graduates have their senior pictures taken in front of the town square statue. Festivals and other activities take place around the statue. The Yancey History Association is justifiably proud of its Otway Burns collection, which includes the entirety of the 1909 dedication speech and many of the references cited herein.

"Brave and honest, faithful to his trust and kind of heart. He was largely generous both in his prosperity and his adversity."

Endnote: We know the words "snap dragon" as an annual flower with a head that resembles the head of a dragon, somewhat.

But this was probably not the origin of Otway Burns' ship's name. As far back as the mid-1500s, a parlor game was played in England named "Snap Dragon." Children and adults sat in a circle on the carpet around a low table that held a large, shallow bowl. Almonds and raisins were placed in the bowl and a liberal amount of brandy was poured over. The brandy was ignited, and the players took turns bobbing for the raisins or reaching into the brandy for a raisin. The other players chanted, "Snip-snap-dragon, snip-snap-dragon." I don't know what made someone the winner of this fiery game—perhaps actually coming up with a raisin!

We know the sloop *Snap Dragon* was quick and very maneuverable, and fire spat from her cannons as she circled her target. As she was very low in the water, she could fire at the water line of ships' hulls while their cannons shot harmlessly over her head. So perhaps this was the origin of the ship's name.

We can only imagine.

THE WREATH IN THE GRAVEYARD

Cataloochee Valley was an old, old community. The first land was registered in 1814. The last resident was moved out 120 years later in 1933. You see, the government wanted land on the western border of North Carolina and the eastern border of Tennessee for a park. It was and is called Great Smoky Mountains National Park. You've heard of it—it's just over beyond Asheville and Cherokee a few miles. Perhaps you've been there to visit, to travel Jonathan Creek and Cove Creek Roads over the mountain, to camp out along Cataloochee Creek, to see the old homesteads and farms.

In the Cataloochee community, there were two churches, Palmer Chapel in Cataloochee, a Methodist congregation, and the Baptist church in Little Cataloochee, some six miles away by road. Palmer Chapel was a fine, strongly built frame church, and the Baptist church was somewhat more primitive. In fact it was called Primitive Baptist Church. It is this church and its graveyard we are going to talk about.

There was a large graveyard there, and in it many of the first families to settle the valley found their final resting place. In the early days, and even up to this day, the families believed in ghosts and haints, and no one would go into the graveyard at night. There was an old rusty iron fence with a gate around the yard made by the ironsmith who had a forge in Little Cataloochee. As long as you stayed outside that fence, no haint would get you, nor could a ghost creep up behind you and follow you home. Many citizens who were scary in life were buried there, and it comes to reason that they were more scary after they were dead. Some of them were just too evil to get into heaven and too mean for the Devil to take in. Therefore, their spirits were restless, sleeping during the daylight hours and rising to roam about the graveyard after dark. You see, they waited for a live person to come by at night and come into the graveyard, then they would enter that person and live through them.

Creeeeepy!

There was a man named Jack Caldwell who lived in Little Cataloochee and he was a brutal man. He was mean to his wife and mean to his kids and he even kicked the poor dog around the yard. And when he got angry, it was a sight to see what meanness he did then. Why, he threw dishes against the wall, tossed the furniture around the room and broke it, and chased his kids into the yard and down the road, shouting and swinging a tree branch after them. One evening he got so mad he was cursing and foaming at the mouth and stomping around on the floor in a dance of fury. He suddenly stopped yelling, looked at his wife in a peculiar way and—fell—down—dead. He had had a stroke in the midst of his anger and died right there! His family did right by him. They buried him in the Little Cataloochee graveyard and had a proper Primitive Baptist funeral for him, although no one there really thought he was going up to heaven and they wondered if even the Devil would take him. Mad Jack was a good candidate for roaming the graveyard at night, they all thought. No one would go into the yard at night for fear that Jack's spirit would catch'em!

When Mad Jack arose from his grave one night, he lurked around the graveyard, just waiting for someone to come by and come in. But no one came, and night after night the haint of Mad Jack lingered around the yard, sighing, hopeful. Then 1933 came, and all the people left for new lives in Tennessee and North Carolina. The Sunday after July the Fourth, was Decoration Day, and every year relatives of the former inhabitants would return to Primitive Baptist Church for a weekend reunion. On Saturday, the community men would clean up the graveyard, weeding and re-mounding dirt over the graves. The women would take crepe paper and pipe cleaners and weave them into dozens of pretty flowers. They then took the flowers and constructed wreaths out of them to lay on the graves of their dead family members. On Sunday, they would gather at the church and have a memorial service for those who had died during the year. After church, the picnic baskets would be retrieved and out would pop fried chicken, potato salad, baked beans, string beans, deviled eggs, apple stack cakes, pound cakes, chocolate cakes and other desserts washed down with mason jars of cold tea fetched from the creek. The food was spread out on tables and shared by all.

Down in the graveyard, Jack's daytime rest was disturbed by the gaiety of people who were reunited after a year's absence, by gossip and the sounds of the enjoyment of good food. He tossed and turned in his casket, muttered to himself, and wished some of those people would come visit during the night. After eating, the gathering walked down to the graveyard to admire the wreaths. Jack heard sounds of walking; some people paused right by his grave. Oh, he wished for nightfall so that he might rise out of the grave at last and inhabit one of them.

But soon the gathering dispersed. Cars and trucks filled with people and left Little Cataloochee. All—except for a young man of sixteen who had been walking down the road searching for an old homestead his uncle had told him about. No one missed him, thinking he was riding with someone else, and so he was left behind. Dusk came, and the young man lingered up at the church, saying out loud to himself, "Well, when they get home they'll find out I'm not there and they will come back for me." So he waited, humming to himself as he strolled down to the graveyard. The moon came out as night fell and illuminated the colorful flowers of the wreaths on the graves. There was something lovely and fetching about them, and not realizing their effect on him, the young man walked through the old iron gate and over to examine the biggest wreath on the grave of Jack Caldwell.

As he stood there, he noticed a strange disturbance of the soil over the grave; it began to tremble and move. The young man watched, transfixed, as the dirt slid back down the sides and the wreath fell off. More dirt slipped away, and the top of the coffin was exposed. It slid open. To his horror, he saw the form of Jack Caldwell rise from the coffin, half decomposed, his clothing hanging in tatters, the flesh rotting from around his face and his hands. Jack stepped out. The hands slowly raised and extended toward the young man, and the body began to stagger toward him. Eyes bulging out of his head, the young man stumbled backwards and fell against another gravestone and into the dirt. Mad Jack advanced. He stood over him, bent down over him, reached for him. The putrid flesh hung just inches from the young man's face.

Lights from a truck illuminated the scene from up on the hill, and someone began to blow the horn and yell. The young man shut his eyes, screamed, and fainted dead away. Men came running down to the graveyard, yelling and throwing rocks. When the young man came to, two men had him by the arms and were dragging him backwards up the hill. He opened one eye, gazed down into the graveyard, and . . . What? Jack was back in the coffin, the dirt was mounded up and smoothed down, and the wreath was back in its place on top of the grave. The young man began blathering, laughing, and howling. No one could understand what he was saying. The men stuffed him into the back seat of the truck cab and they left, burning rubber up the dirt road

Down in the graveyard, Jack turned over in his coffin and sighed.

JACK TALE

The Jack Tale story genre is not indigenous to Appalachia. Jack is well-traveled, sailing to the New World with the earliest settlers from Ireland, Wales, England, and Scotland. If you know "Jack and the Beanstalk," you know Jack. And you know him as a sometimes-lazy boy, but always clever and looking for a slick deal with the least amount of expended energy. He settled in the Southern Appalachians and we are glad to claim him.

This is an original Jack Tale I wrote.

JACK OUT AWHILE IN THE WORLD

Well now, Jack was a'sittin' out on the cabin porch one day, not doin' much an' feelin' kinder bored. He was reared back against the wall in a cane-bottom chair, just cogitatin'. His mind drifted along 'til it fixed on the idear that he should jus' walk out awhile in the world an' see what he could see. So he told his mama he'd see her long 'bout suppertime an' he set off walkin'. He walked through his home county, come to the settle-ment whar they's a general store, a porch on the front, an' a bench on the porch, an' three girls a'settin' on the bench. Them girls started gigglin' an' twitterin'.

"Why, hello thar Jack. Whar you off to?"

"Nowhar in partic'lar—just amblin."

"Are ye a'goin' off to Giant Land today?"

"Naw."

"Are ye gonna find ye a yunycorn?"

"Naw."

"Are ye gonna to marry up with a king's daughter?"

"Well, iffen I run up on one."

Them was some irritatin' girls, an' he pulled off on down the county road. An' he walked into the next county. He was in a walkin' frame o'mind. An' he walked into the next county, an' it looked a bit strange to him. He come up on a little goat track led off into the woods, an' he turned off. He walked a piece more an' come up on a little cabin an' hallooed at it. Ye gotta halloo or yer britches might get dusted by a little bird-shot. He was getting' a mite bit thirsty an' hungry too, by now. A little ole wizenedy woman come out on the front porch an' peered down at him.

"Why looky hyar; it's a half-starved young'un. Ye better come in now an' have some soup with me."

Jack said, "Why that's mighty good-natured of ye an' yes'em, I'll come in an' eat some soup." He went in after the woman, saw there was a big, black iron kettle steamin' away on a hook swung over the fire.

"Mmmm, why that smells like some kinda good soup."

"Why, yes, I put some good thangs in it that just turn up. Like this mornin', I went out back to the garden patch an' turned up some turnips, an onion, an' some taters. I looked for the carrots but the tops'd died back an' I couldn't find 'em."

"I'll go out thar an' I'll find ye some carrots." He took a shovel from the porch, went 'round back to the garden patch. He found them carrots an' dug'em up. He brought them in the cabin. The ole woman scraped an' sliced 'em an' threw 'em in the pot. Mmmm, that soup was smellin' good now. "Is it time to eat?" he asked.

"Soon's I get a little side meat to go in. But ye can get warshed up."

She put another kettle on the fire, a little'un. She took a penknife an' a chunk of lye soap offen the shelf an' shaved some slivers into the kettle. Soon them soap bubbles was risin' into the air an' going *POP! POP!* all 'round the cabin, an' Jack 'llowed it was a purty sight— them little round rainbows floatin' all 'round.

He warshed his hands an' face an' the ole woman said, "Just take yer shirt off an' warsh yer uppers."

Jack took off his shirt, peeled his longjohns off down to the waist an' warshed his uppers.

"Ye could roll up yer pants legs an' warsh yer lowers."

Well, Jack had not had a bath in a week so he allowed this was a good opportunity an' he rolled up the overalls an' underwear an' warshed them lowers. He didn't worry none 'bout his middles—they'd been good an' covered up.

That soup was smellin' mighty good an' he was really gettin' hungry. Jack heard steps comin' up behind him. He looked around an' that ole woman was advancin' on 'im with a big butcher's knife. Why, he'd never seen a knife so big.

"Why, watch out thar, ye could get hurt!" he hollared.

"Ain't me's gonna get hurt. I told ye I needed some side meat an' thar's some nice clean side meat, right thar!" An' she poked that knife right at his ribs.

"Well now, I can go catch us a whistle pig or a possum fer some side meat an' nobody gets hurt." Jack was thinkin' quick, figurin' he could get out of that cabin, hungry as he was, an' make a run for it. But that soup was a'smellin' so good.

"Hmmm," said the ole woman, "I reckon I could do with a pig or a possum."

So Jack went an' made him a slip-noose trap an' staked it out in front of a whistle pig hole out back. Terrectly, that ole earth whistle pig come home an' stepped right in it an' it tightened up 'round his laig. Oh, he pulled an' he pulled an' he whistled an' he whistled an' thar's no help fer him. Jack came an' knocked him up the side o'the haid an' laid him out. The old woman took the whistle pig, skinned an' butchered him an' popped him into the soup.

In jus' a little while the soup was ready, the ole woman laid the knife up, an' Jack 'llowed as how he should jus' stay an' git his lunch. He an' the ole woman ate an' parted as friends. Jack with his uppers, lowers, middles, an' side meat in one piece pulled on down the county road.

Jack walked awhile on an' come to another cabin. Thar was a man an' a woman a'sittin' outside on the porch. Jack thought that was a little odd, seein' as how thar was corn in the field to harvest an' the chickens was a'runnin' around cluckin'. They's beggin' to be fed, an' a cow was a-bellerin' in the barn, pore ole thang. Thar was no smoke comin' out the chimney an' obviously no victuals a'cookin'. Jack stopped an' hallooed at them.

"Come right on in the yard," hollered the man. "We been a-waitin' on ye."

"Waitin' on ME? How did ye know I was a-comin'?"

"Aw, they's always someone a-comin'," said the woman. "Here we are, ole an' lame, an' not much good fer nothin'. The corn's in the field an' needs to be picked, that ole cow needs a'milkin' an' the chicks ain't been fed yet today. Can ye help us?"

"Well, that's a lot o' work," said Jack, fer he was not much into corn-pickin', cow-milkin', an' chicken-feedin'. "I think ye'll have to give me something awful good fer all that."

"Well, how would twenty dollars do?"

"Why, that'd be a most handsome sum." Jack, who'd never seen twenty dollars in his life, set in to milkin' the cow first to hesh her up. Then he threw shelled corn to the chickens. He asked the man fer his wagon an' horse, hitched'em up, an' drove out into the corn field. Before too long, he had picked that field clean an' returned to the cabin.

"I'm done now an' want my pay," he said to the couple who was still sittin' on the porch. Jack was thinking of what all he could buy with that twenty dollars.

"Sure, my boy, yew just sit here on the porch with the ole man an' I'll go in an' git it," said the woman.

Jack peeked in the winder after her an' saw'er take an ole purse outta a drawer in a chifforobe. She opened it an' there was a huge, I mean huge, wad o'money. Jack's eyes bulged out an' he started thinkin' how to git it—all of it.

The woman come back out an' handed Jack a twenty an' a five. "That extry's fer workin' so fast," she said.

"Why, thanky. Is there anything else I can do fer you'uns?"

"Well, ye can take this here money into town an' put it in the bank fer us. We was talkin' 'bout how you 'pear to be an honest an' hard-workin' boy. All them others who come by was a disappointment to us—not good for nuthin'. But you're a good boy an' ye can see we cain't get to town on our own. Jus' set out on this here road an' keep a'goin'."

Jack thought, *Now ain't that jus' nice; they think I'm an honest person. I cain't steal their money with'em thinkin' that way 'bout me. Dang it!* He took the huge wad of money, stuffed it in his overall's pocket an' set out for town an' the bank.

He walked on an' walked on. Then he come to the settle-ment. Hmm, hit looked a bit familiar. He saw a general store an' there was a porch on the front an' a bench on the porch an' there was three girls a'sittin' on that bench. It was the same store an' porch an' bench an' girls he had seen earlier that morning.

Why, he had jus walked around in a big ole circle!

Them girls hollered at him, "Well now, Jack, tell us about yore 'ventures today."

They was some irritatin' girls. He threw 'em a sour look an' marched on down the street to the bank where he deposited the money, less his twenty-five dollars, into the bank fer the ole couple. The manager's eyes popped out on stalks seein' that wad o'cash! He called the bank presydent outter his office to handle the transaction. The presydent came out an' gasped at the amount: $2,527! That brought the bank's assets up to the princely sum o' $3,043.72. He offered Jack a job as loan officer in trainin' on the very spot.

Now, the last I heard, Jack had made bank vice presydent. Them overalls is hangin' on a peg. He wears suits now from the Sears Roebuck an' brogan shoes. He bathes twice a week. On Saturdays, he goes out to the couple's cabin, picks the corn, milks the cow, an' feeds the chickens. It's the least he can do.

Oh an' he's been thinkin' that maybe, one day, he jus' might marry up with one o' them irritatin' girls.

REFERENCES

Barbour, Ruth P. *Cruise of the Snap Dragon.* John F. Blair. Winston-Salem, North Carolina, 197.

Burns, Frances. *Captain Otway Burns: Patriot, Privateer, Legislator.* Collected and Compiled. New York, 1905.

Conrad, Dennis, PhD. Address before the Carolina Mountain Literacy Festival. Burnsville, North Carolina, September 2008.

Daniels, Josephus. *The Wilson Years of Peace: 1910-1917.* Chapel Hill Press. Chapel Hill, North Carolina, 1944.

Dye, Ira. "American Maritime Prisoners of War 1812-1815." *Ships, Seafaring, and Society.* Maryland State Archives.

ABOUT THE AUTHOR

A lifelong storyteller, Catherine Yael Serota Shealy was first published at age twelve in the UNC-Asheville publication, Laurel. Today, her storytelling portfolio contains tales of Appalachian history, folk tales, tall tales, personal vignettes, and literary masterpieces seasoned with humor. She holds degrees from five universities in subjects ranging from concert piano and European History to counseling and theology.

As a professional storyteller, Catherine has performed at Asheville's Front Porch, TELLABRATION!™, Blue Ridge Storytelling Summit, Stone Soup Festival, Mountain Makins Festival, house concerts, synagogues, the Hendersonville Center for Art and Inspiration, and corporate and therapeutic venues. She is a member of the National Storytelling Network, NC Guild, Asheville Storytelling Circle, and a performing member of the Jonesborough Storytellers Guild.

Some of her fondest memories are of time spent with her mother collecting plant samples in the forests of the Southern Highlands, writing legislation in North Carolina for funding to support survivors of domestic violence and sexual assault, and the twenty-five years she spent owning and operating Glenfiddich Christmas Tree Farm and Nursery in Haywood County, North Carolina, where she designed and built a hand-hewn poplar log house with her first husband, Bob Scott.

Catherine and her husband, Wallace, now live in a small mountain town in Tennessee when they aren't out of state birdwatching or on one of their "go-look-see" trips.